Creative Aging
52 Ways to Add Life to Your Years

Carol Van Klompenburg

Copyright © 2023 Carol Van Klompenburg

All rights reserved.

ISBN: 9798393566272

Dedication

To my late father, Henry Addink, and others of his generation who served as models for creative aging.

Contents

Dedication iii
Contents v
Acknowledgments viii
1 Not Yet Old 1
2 On Memory Lane 5
3 Discovering Ageism 9
4 On Bonding 13
5 Weathering Loss 17
6 The Good Old Days 21
7 Taking Retirement 25
8 Faster and Faster 29
9 Is Age Just a Number? 33
10 Better with Age 37
11 A Purpose in Life 41
12 A Sound Mind in a Sound Body 45
13 Brain Workouts 49
14 Sharpened by Community 53
15 Movies for Seniors 57
16 Words from the Old Days 61
17 The Child Within 65
18 OK, Google 69
19 Five Kinds of Wealth 73
20 Our Youth-Oriented Culture 77
21 On Fatigue and Grandchildren 81
22 Retirement Guilt Trip 85

23 The Care and Feeding of Your Soul............ 89
24 How to Make a Financial Retirement Plan... 93
25 Charitable Use of Individual Retirement Accounts.. 97
26 Senior Scams 101
27 Pangs While Purging................................. 105
28 Lighting Small Corners 109
29 The Aging of the Boomer Bubble............... 113
30 On Antiques and Aging............................ 117
31 Senior Moment Debate 121
32 The Best Years 125
33 The Importance of Balance 129
34 To Laugh or Not to Laugh 133
35 In Praise of Naps 137
36 Play to Win?... 141
37 The Organized Mind 145
38 After the Fall 149
39 High Tech, Low Control 153
40 Family Clowns.. 157
41 Losing Multitasking Skills 161
42 Phone Call.. 165
43 The Great Unretirement........................... 169
44 Accepting Limits...................................... 173
45 On Pride and Technology......................... 177
46 The Benefits of Writing Your Story............ 181
47 How to Start Writing Your Memories......... 185
48 How to Polish and Publish Your Writing ... 189
49 Coping Devices for Aging Losses 193

50 For Further Reading 197
51 Happy Retirees 201
52 Commencement 205
About the Author 209

Acknowledgments

Thank you to:

- Pella Writing Group for feedback and suggestions for every chapter: Lee Collins, Bob Hutzell, Deb Jansen, Helen Luhrs, Anne Petrie, and Mary Beth Wigginton.

- To Steve Woodhouse for running the columns in the *Marion County Express.*

- To Doug Calsbeek for running the columns in the *Sioux County Capital Democrat.*

1 Not Yet Old

Denial ain't just a river in Egypt. –Mark Twain

My first complimentary issue of *AARP The Magazine* arrived on my 50th birthday. *Why on earth is the American Association of Retired Persons sending this to ME?* I wondered. *I am at least 15 years from retirement. I'm definitely and solidly in midlife.*

I grumbled to my husband and tossed it into the recycling bin, unopened. Each month a new issue arrived. For a year, each issue suffered the same fate.

That was more than two decades ago. No matter which birthday I celebrated after that, I was sure old age still lurked 10 to 15 years down the road.

Age is just a number, I thought. *I am unusually healthy and very active for my stage of life.* I bought a pickleball racket and joined a local drop-in group, sure my tennis background qualified me to compete with women a decade or two younger than me.

Two years ago, I decided to research the aging process, to prepare for the future date in which I began to age. I was not yet old, but if I did the math, I could not deny that, even if I lived to be 100, I was in the final third of my life.

I googled aging, successful aging, senior living, healthy aging, and many more terms. I also googled "best books on aging." I ordered interlibrary loan books, put e-books on my Kindle, and stacked paperbacks on my shelves. Some books depressed me; others encouraged me. In many forms, I confronted this fact: Aging is inevitable, and many people try to ignore the process.

Some books did imply you could reverse the aging process and seemingly live forever, or at least to a very, very, very old age. But those books didn't ring true for me. They were usually promoting some miracle product.

Muriel Gillick confronted those books and me. In *Denial of Aging,* she wrote, "We would like to think that if we eat nutritious meals and exercise faithfully, we will be able to fend off old age. When we believe we will stay young forever, and when we purchase special vitamins, herbs, and other youth-enhancing chemicals to promote longevity, we are engaging in massive denial."

I thought of the vegetarian diet I was experimenting with and the assorted capsules in my medicine cabinet. I was helping anti-aging products break sales records each consecutive year. In 2020, the global anti-aging market was estimated to be 58.5 billion US dollars, and it will likely see a compound annual growth rate of 7 percent between 2021 and 2026.

In my reading I learned 30 percent of Americans would rather not think about getting older at all. Their denial might arise from pride, embarrassment, fear, or depression. I learned most of us have a younger self-image than our actual age; we think everyone our age looks older than we do. I winced. Just the day before I had glimpsed a woman in a store window, wondered who that old woman was, and realized with a shock I was looking at my reflection.

I learned older adults tend to dissociate themselves from their peers when negative stereotypes become prominent. *Yes,* I thought, *I withdraw emotionally from conversations when peers begin their organ recitals of their latest medical complications.*

The mass of evidence convinced me: I am an older person. It also convinced me "older" is a gentler way to describe my age than "old." I learned I would be guilty of ageism if I used the terms "elderly" or "over the hill." But that's a topic for another column.

Seeing myself as part of the older generation has been a paradigm shift for me. It's as if continental drift has happened overnight. The landmass of my youth has been split off from me, not over millions of years, but in an instant.

I am continuing my research. I want to know all I can about my current stage of life: how to enjoy the new freedoms, how to cope with the losses, how to find new sources of identity, etc.

As a lifelong writer, I have decided to do what I have always done with significant changes in my life: write about it. With that decision a book has been born: *Creative Aging.*

Together, in each chapter we will explore this new adolescence in which we ask ourselves who we will be as we grow older. We will journey through the ups and downs, the pluses and minuses of this new stage of life. We will look at how to successfully adapt to our changing selves. And we'll have the grace to laugh at ourselves along the way.

Welcome aboard!

2 On Memory Lane

You need three umbrellas: one to leave at a friend's house, one to leave at home, and one to leave everywhere else.

It happened again just last week. After an acquaintance had told me she enjoyed reading my memoir, *Child of the Plains,* she said, "I also enjoyed another book lately. It was written by—" and she paused.

"Oh, darn," she said, "I can't remember her name. She does the one-woman performances about Mareah Scholte, the wife of Pella's founder."

"Beverly Graves?" I asked.

"Yes, that's it!" she said. "This 83-year-old brain doesn't work so well."

She criticized her brain function, but it had worked on three out of four fronts. She remembered enjoying the book, she could describe the author, and she recognized the name when I said it. Three out of four isn't bad; it's like a batting average of 750.

She was simply having a moment when her brain synapses clicked into pause mode. And research reveals that pause mode already begins happening to people in their mid-thirties. It simply happens a bit more often to older people. I reassured her I sometimes have trouble remembering as well. "I have a photographic memory," I told her. "But occasionally my camera lacks film."

Sociologists have made studies of brain-film effectiveness. One study showed complex pictures to both younger and older people and asked them for a narration about everything they saw. The older people made more mistakes in naming items as they narrated.

However, when asked simply to name each item in a series of one-item pictures, the older people did better than the younger ones. Semantic memory, our knowledge of words, numbers, and general concepts, improves with age.

Our procedural memory remains unchanged. So older adults can generally remember how to cook an omelet, tell time on a clock, tie a bow, or type as well as they ever could.

Some of our abilities remain strong, but they slow down. Older adults process information more slowly and require more repetition to learn something new. It also takes us more time to shift focus from one task to another. So, it is wise for us to stay focused on one task at a time rather than trying to multi-task.

One memory that declines with age is episodic memory—the what, where, and when of daily life. That memory decline is the reason I sometimes ask my husband to call my smartphone to help me find it. It is the reason I have difficulty recalling what I ate for lunch yesterday.

Our attitudes influence our memories. The more anxiety I experience when I try to remember a name, the further the name retreats. I have one friend who is good at saying calmly, "I'm drawing a blank on that right now. It will come to me later." Another friend says simply, "Hmm. I'm having a mental pause." And then my friends move on to another topic, or to telling the story they were going to tell, minus the name that momentarily disappeared. When I relax and move on, often the name comes back to me when I am no longer trying to think of it.

One source of our anxiety is the worry we are developing dementia, a fairly widespread fear in later years according to psychologists. I comfort myself with a reminder, "Forgetting where I put my phone is normal. Forgetting what the phone is for is not." Statistics are in our favor. Fewer than one in five people over 65, and less than half of those over 85, have Alzheimer's disease. Besides, worrying about the future accomplishes nothing except to darken the present. (If you are forgetting how to do daily tasks or missing important appointments, though, you might want to consult with your physician.)

A positive attitude, instead of a negative one, allows us to master new skills. We CAN learn a new language; it simply requires a little additional time and repetition. We CAN learn acrylic painting, playing piano, or woodworking. We simply need to allow ourselves time to develop the skill. And retirement living allows us the luxury of extra time.

There are coping skills for some of the declines. When trying to remember a name, my husband cycles through the alphabet for a beginning letter that seems to belong with the missing name. Sometimes if he comes up with a first letter, I can retrieve the name. We joke that between the two of us we have a complete brain. However, when we get into our car, he has never said to me, "Okay, I will remember where we are going. You remember who we are."

Sometimes, when I walk into a room and can't remember what I went there for, I can retrieve the memory by returning to the room I started from. Sometimes that doesn't help, and I simply go on with life. If it was important, it will occur to me again. Simply going on is a healthier choice than being convinced for some reason I am going to find a clue in the refrigerator.

Older people also cope with misplaced items when we do what our grandmothers preached: establish a place for everything and put everything in its place. Marlo and I always park in the same section of the church parking lot. I have learned a fanny pack is wonderful for keeping track of my smart phone. (A belt clip or pocket would also work.) My keys have a permanent home in a zippered compartment of my purse.

Lest I forget to mention it, there are techniques for maintaining, and even improving memory. But that's a topic for another column.

And now if I could just remember where I put my glasses.

3 Discovering Ageism

I've learned that life is like a roll of toilet paper: The closer it gets to the end, the faster it goes. –Andy Rooney

Talk about getting old! I was getting dressed, and a Peeping Tom looked in the window, took a look—and pulled down the shade. –Joan Rivers

Let's begin with a question. I think one of the above jokes is ageist. Which one is it?

Another question first: What's ageism? Although the term was coined in 1968 by physician Robert Butler, I hadn't heard the term until I started researching aging a few years ago.

Ageism is a prejudice, like racism or sexism. According to Butler, it is a process of systematic stereotyping of and discrimination against people because they are old.

Which joke is ageist? Joan Rivers' joke depends on the stereotype that older people are unattractive.

I must admit, though, when I classify Joan Rivers' joke as ageist, a skeptic at the back of my brain thinks, *Give me a break. It's just a joke!*

But the experts tell me negative stereotypes are hurtful to older people. Our self-perceptions can be shaped by what we hear repeatedly. And a University of Michigan National Poll revealed 82 percent of adults aged 50 to 80 experience one or more forms of ageism daily.

Ageism occurs in more than jokes. It happens in word choice and behaviors as well.

AARP The Magazine classified the following terms for older people as ageist: elderly, adorable, of a certain age, over the hill, blue-hairs, little old lady, old coot, geezer, fogey, codger, and even senior citizen.

Wait a minute, I thought when reading the list, *Senior Citizen is an ageist term? Why?* So, I dug deeper and learned the term "citizen" tends to be associated more with numbers than with humanity. *OK, I can see that. Sort of. But for me that is a bit of a stretch. To me the term just seems unnecessarily formal.*

My other response to the list was *Goodness! What terms CAN I use?* AARP had a list for that as well: older, experienced, wise, seasoned, sage, mature, perennial, ageless, vintage, and distinguished.

Hmm. Some of those terms work for me, and some seem a bit of a stretch. I can't see myself calling an older person perennial. To me that is a plant term for a flower that comes up year after year. And vintage is a term I reserve for clothing and antiques. Applied to people, these terms feel a bit clunky.

I decided I was most comfortable with the term "older people," and probably would likely use that most often.

I scanned the two lists again and realized I question some of the terms in both lists, but I do have a much more negative feeling about being an older person after reading the first list than the second one.

Sally Brown of the Vital Aging Network says some examples of ageist behavior and products are so common—and sometimes well-meaning—we might not even think of them as ageist:
- Birthday parties featuring black balloons and over-the-hill gifts. I think back to some over-the-

hill gift-giving. *Hmm. The laughter of the recipient of some of those gag gifts was sometimes embarrassed and nervous. It was not a pleasure-filled belly laugh.*
- Anti-aging products. *When I read ads for anti-aging products, I regard my maturity as something negative. As a result, I dislike what I see in the mirror.*
- Assuming young people are computer geniuses and older people are technologically inept. *When I assume my technology skills are lacking, I make it more difficult to master them. Not a good idea!*

As I researched ageism, I realized: *I am among the 36 percent of older people who have internalized ageist biases.*

I also realized: *I can change, but it will take time.*

What about you? Are you with me in discovering hidden ageist bias in yourself? Did you spot the ageism in the Joan Rivers joke? Would you like a second chance? Here are two more jokes.

When you are dissatisfied and would like to go back to youth, think of algebra. –Will Rogers.

Whatever you may look like, marry a man your own age. As your beauty fades, so will his eyesight. –Phyllis Diller.

May you identify and resist each ageist messages you see and hear!

4 On Bonding

There isn't time, so brief is life, for bickering, apologies, heart burnings, callings to account. There is only time for loving, and but an instant, so to speak, for that. –Mark Twain

Those who love deeply never grow old. They may die of old age, but they die young. –Benjamin Franklin

"She was sobbing, so I walked over to her and gave her a big hug," said Kathryn. She volunteers as a receptionist one day per week at an Iowa social service agency that offers help to people in hard places. "Now each week when she comes in, she talks with me before she goes to her counseling session."

Kathryn had begun a relationship. Her face was radiant as she told me the story. That new relationship brought her joy.

But good relationships—whether marital, family, or social—don't bring just joy. A Harvard Study tracked 724 men for 75 years and generated tens of thousands of pages of information. The study's clearest message: good relationships keep us happier and healthier.

The expanding field of neuroscience teaches us that people with social support generally have better mental health, heart health, immune systems, and brain function.

In his book *Timeless,* psychology professor Louis Cozolino writes that our brains are social organs, and so we are wired to connect with others and be part of groups. We are like trees in a farm grove; we look like individual trees, but deep underground the roots that nourish and feed us are intertwined.

In the 1960s, researchers believed that social relationships become impaired and less satisfying with age. However, more recent research shows just the opposite. In general, older adults typically report higher levels of satisfaction with their social relationships than younger adults.

Our social circles may shrink a bit as some of our friends die or move away, but our networks are also smaller by our own choice. We may reduce contact with some acquaintances and maintain ties with closer friends and partners. We keep the relationships that are most rewarding. For close relationships, it is wise to show gratitude and never take those you love for granted.

While good relationships benefit our health, loneliness can be deadly. It increases mortality by 26 percent according to one study cited in *Perspectives in Psychological Science.* And more than one in five Americans is lonely at some point.

One explanation for the increased mortality among lonely people is that social relationships help reduce our stress and lower our level of the stress hormone cortisol, which is hard on our bodies and our emotions.

One transition that can produce loneliness is retirement, when you no longer see the same network of people at work every day. It takes effort to replace workmates with playmates. Other transitions, such as moving or a change in your physical status that limits your participation in a previously enjoyed activity, can also produce loneliness. Or perhaps you are one of the world's introverts who doesn't build relationships easily. What can you do?

If you find yourself staring at the television more hours than is good for you, you may want to replace screen time with people time.

Volunteering, as my friend Kathryn did, is one way to build bonds with new people. Opportunities to volunteer abound: churches, schools, soup kitchens, libraries, rescue missions, thrift stores, and more.

Building a relationship with grandchildren or other youth can boost our morale. The bond between young and old is a special treasure. Colozino says, "We build the brains of our children through our interaction with them, and we keep our own brains growing and changing throughout life by staying connected with others."

It's also wise, at this stage of life, to establish a strong relationship with a good physician.

The bonds we establish can be with friends, family members, or spouses. What is critical is to have a network of loving relationships with people who are there for us when we need them.

As my friend Kathryn learned, relationships in which we provide support for others are some of the most rewarding bonds. I volunteer weekly at that same reception desk as Kathryn. I like the way Kathryn's face glowed when she talked about the new bond that had grown. In the future, I would like to be more sensitive to the needs of the clients I welcome. It just might contribute to their health—and mine.

5 Weathering Loss

You know you're getting older when you're told to slow down by your doctor, instead of by the police. —Joan Rivers

Although aging brings us new opportunities and insights, it also brings losses. And the list of those potential losses is discouragingly long. It includes loss of physical abilities, of property, of people and relationships, along with mental and emotional losses. And each of these categories has multiple examples.

That's the bad news. Here are the silver linings. Not all older people experience all possible kinds of loss. And losses don't come all at once; they often accumulate gradually. By the time we reach our senior years, we have probably had significant practice at coping with loss. When I married, I lost a certain independence. When I had infants and toddlers, I lost my weekends off. One loss was monumental: In 2017, my youngest son died of an opiate overdose.

Perhaps, remembering those past losses, we can gather strength to deal with life's current losses as well. Adjusting may require some grieving, but I have learned tears are the pressure valve that releases sadness, anxiety, and even fear. After sessions of tears over the loss of my son, I had more strength to walk through the next steps in a day. As months passed by,

I gradually learned that it is possible to be happy again, even after loss. Life did not need to be perfect to include joy. As Karl Pillemer said, "We learn to be happy in spite of, not happy if only."

If we allow it, pain can produce growth. It doesn't happen immediately. It doesn't justify the pain or make it go away, but it is growth nonetheless. Pain can soften our hearts and make us more sensitive to the sufferings of others. Pain can humble us so that we realize our need for others. Pain can make us vulnerable and open to being loved.

But pain and loss do not automatically produce growth. They can make us bitter or they can make us better. We have a choice. That principle is essential for Viktor Frankl in *Man's Search for Meaning*.

Frankl did not just spin theory. He lived with great loss as a prisoner in a Nazi concentration camp during World War II. His mother, father, brother, and wife all died in the camps. His captors took from him almost every element of personal value and human dignity.

The only thing they were not able to take was his choice of how to respond. He described that response as "the last of the human freedoms—to choose one's attitude in any given set of circumstances, to choose one's own way."

Chronic pain treatment focuses on the difference between pain and suffering. Some pain is unavoidable, but suffering can be avoided. Suffering occurs when we think *Why me? This is more than I can bear. This is terrible.* We can make the choice not to suffer. We can radically accept the life we are given.

Six years ago, when I discussed my son's addictions with my therapist, she asked me, "If the worst possible thing happened, could you survive?"

I paused for a long time and said slowly, "I think I could. It would hurt like hell, but I think I could." I had survived giving birth to a stillborn son, and eventually found joy in spite of loss. I trusted I would be given strength to survive whatever pain the future might hold. Over time I did receive that strength.

Mary Pipher says in *Women Rowing North*, "Great personal suffering can sometimes deepen our souls to the point they crack open and let in great beauty."

She says that when our hearts crack open, we identify with all who have suffered, and we pray not only for ourselves but for everyone who has suffered. She adds that happiness doesn't happen because we are problem-free but because we have learned to be present to the moment.

She concludes, "Yet, in spite of our situations, whatever they are, we all can have our days when we feel like a three-legged cat, drenched in sunlight."

As we age, we may be like three-legged cats, but we can take pleasure in the warmth and beauty of the sun.

6 The Good Old Days

My grandfather is always saying that in the old days people could leave their back doors open. Which is probably why his submarine sank. –Milton Jones, Comedian

It happened again last week. I was part of a group of older people who began to reminisce about their childhoods. The conversation turned to party-line telephones and people who rubbernecked. (They listened in on other people's conversations.) It included recalling what your particular ring was: one-long-and-two-shorts or short-long-short or some other long-short ring combination. Your phone rang whenever someone on your party line was being called, and you knew if it was for you by distinguishing the longs and the shorts. They talked about how the world had changed—to private lines with cordless phones, then cell phones, and then smartphones.

I was part of that group, but I said nothing. I thought—somewhat judgmentally I confess—that we were sounding like a bunch of old fogies. (Yes, I used that ageist term. Sorry.)

On our daily walks, when my husband sometimes reminisces about his childhood Go-Kart or his Doodlebug mini-bike, I listen, but I do not chime in with my own memories of playing Kick the Can or

Eenie Einie Over.

Increasingly, my peers have been reminiscing, while I listen—and sometimes judge.

Should I? When my father was in his final months, the hospice social workers sometimes asked him about his past, encouraging him to reminisce.

I googled "reminiscing" and was surprised by what I learned.

I learned that we start reminiscing around age 10. Young people and older people reminisce more than people at midlife, perhaps because midlife people tend to have less discretionary time.

I discovered that perhaps my negative attitude was out of date. In the early 1900s, reminiscing by older people was disparaged as an unhealthy dysfunction. Then in 1963, aging expert Robert Butler maintained that reminiscing was universal and natural—and could be positive. He called it "life review."

I found post-1963 articles that were over-the-top in their praise of reminiscing: They said it preserves family history, improves quality of life, reduces depression, promotes physical health, eliminates boredom, improves communication skills, reduces stress, enhances self-esteem, and more.

But still I wondered, remembering times when my older relatives angrily rehearsed old hurts. Is all reminiscing good? Then I found a balanced viewpoint that rang true for me. In the 1990s, psychologists Lisa Watt and Paul Wong classified different types of reminiscing.

- Obsessive: "Everything was terrible."
- Escapist: "Those were the glory days."
- Narrative: "This is what happened."
- Transmissive: "When I was your age. . ."
- Instrumental: "I conquered hardship. I can do it again."
- Integrative: "My life had worth."

They then evaluated the effect of each kind of reminiscing and found different effects.

- Obsessive: When we remember how awful some events were and stay stuck there, we fail to incorporate them into a meaningful life and feel bad all over again.
- Escapist: Although it can defend our egos, remembering the good old days as better than the present is generally not healthy. It can reduce satisfaction with our current life.
- Narrative: Watt and Wong reached no conclusions about the positive or negative effect of our telling a story about the past factually without coloring or interpreting it.
- Instrumental: When we tell a story of surviving hardship in the past, we enhance our feelings of strength and competence. These stories include achieving goals despite barriers, and we draw from them to overcome present problems.
- Integrative: When I review the story of my life and evaluate it as having value, I feel good about myself. These stories can include reconciling the difference between the ideal and reality, accepting negative life events, and resolving old conflicts.

Watt and Wong convinced me that some kinds of reminiscing are indeed good. And, though I fall silent when a group starts reminiscing, I do reminisce in other ways—and some of it has been good for me. After I had written *Child of the Plains: A Memoir,* I found, to my surprise that I had made peace with some painful experiences of my childhood. When my grandchildren ask for an old-days bedtime story, and I tell them about being a five-year-old afraid to ride on a different school bus seat from my brother but doing it anyway, I feel good afterwards.

I have begun work writing for my heirs the stories of

the mementos and artwork around my house. I am realizing through that process that also in my adult life are stories I find worth sharing.

My friends' conversation about party-line phones was not escapist. They weren't reliving glory days. They were simply narrating stories about the way things used to be different.

Maybe, just maybe, when the reminiscing is not escapist or obsessive, I can find a good story to share the next time a group of my friends begins to reminisce.

7 Taking Retirement

When people retire and time is no longer crucial, their colleagues present them with a watch.

When I was in my early sixties and I saw friends retiring, I was jealous. That jealousy was a huge shift for me. Three decades earlier, at retirement parties, I had pitied the retirees. "They must feel abandoned," I thought. "They are like ancient horses, being put out to pasture. This is a time to mourn, not a time to laugh."

Now, at 63, I thought the grass in that pasture looked lush and green. I was weary of managing the Write Place, a writing and graphic arts service I had launched 20 years earlier. What started out as a fascinating challenge became a wearying grind. I had more energy for a business start-up than for ongoing management.

So, when a talented member of my staff agreed to take over management for me, I was ecstatic. I thought, "Finally I will be able to linger over a morning cup of coffee, enjoy the cardinals and finches at the feeder, and putter in my flower gardens. My happily-ever-after has begun!"

I enjoyed the slow pace for several months, but

there was a limit to the amount of lingering and puttering my Type-A personality could enjoy. Life felt hollow.

While working, I had scrounged my days to find time; now I hunted for activities to fill them. I tried exotic coffees, I added new bird feeders, I added flowerbeds, but the emptiness remained. I was contributing very little to the larger world.

In my reading, I have learned my experience was not unusual. A honeymoon phase is typical for people who have grown weary of their jobs. However, for those who have left jobs that still felt fulfilling or been forced to retire earlier than they hoped, the emptiness may be immediate.

Studies show retirement is also tougher if we have made sacrifices in our personal lives for the sake of our jobs.

Retirement, like other major life changes, introduces stress into our lives. It ranks tenth on the Life Change Index Scale. It produces less stress than the death of a family member, but more stress than the death of a close friend.

Some people choose to delay retirement rather than deal with the stress. I know one man who kept working at the same company till he turned 83. He had no children and no hobbies. He liked his work and feared if he retired, he would die. So, he happily kept working.

Others choose to ease the transition with "bridge jobs," often part-time. Some continue at their current company. Others find different, less demanding work. A school principal I know now works as a checkout clerk at a grocery store. He gets to see the parents and children he knew while at school.

Like me, some people find those first weeks exhilarating. They do the home improvement project they have wanted to. They take that dream vacation. They sleep in, linger over the morning paper, and join other retirees for coffee at a local restaurant.

In the long run, though, too much free time can eventually produce the same symptoms as overwork: anxiety, depression, appetite loss, memory impairment, and insomnia.

What is a retiree to do?

I chose volunteering. I volunteered at The Work of Our Hands, a local fair-trade store. I thought it would be a good match for my interest in global justice.

My first assignment: work the retail floor. I trained under a fellow volunteer. She greeted customers warmly as they entered. I envied her friendly charm. I watched them warm to her instantly. "There is no way I can do that!" I thought. "I am invading their space. When I shop, I like to be left alone! Introvert that I am, I could never achieve such instant warmth."

The manager put me to work in the back room, applying price stickers—not a good match for a perfectionist with five-thumb hands.

I whimpered to the manager, "Do you by any chance have a writing job you need done?"

Yes, she did. The store newsletter had languished for lack of a writer. I grabbed the opportunity. It matched.

It had taken several false starts, but I had found a niche.

Volunteering is not the only retiree option, however. The solutions for using time are many. They include taking a class, finding a part-time job, starting a new hobby, or taking an old hobby to a higher level.

Whatever we choose, we can expect peaks and valleys in retirement living. I was wrong to picture it as happily ever after. Life is no fairy tale. Retirement is just normal life in a different stage with new challenges and new opportunities.

8 Faster and Faster

How did it get so late so soon?
It's night before it's afternoon.
December is here before it's June.
My goodness, how the time has flewn.
How did it get so late so soon?"
—Dr. Seuss

"When I look back these days, time has traveled faster," said a friend of mine in an older social group. "When I was a kid, it took forever to get from one Christmas to the next. Now they seem to come one right after the other."

Around the room, we smiled and nodded. We had all felt it. Time seems to go faster each year.

"Why is that?" someone asked.

None of us knew.

Birthdays and anniversaries recur with amazing speed. We blink our eyes and our grandchildren have gained year, then suddenly they graduate from college.

But it's not just the years that fly by. Brushing my teeth last week, I looked over at my husband who was doing the same, and I said, "I don't understand. It seems I did this just an hour ago!"

At my 50th class reunion, I was aghast at the

crow's-feet, the gray or bald heads, and the thickened waistlines. How could that happen so fast? It had been just a few years since we were students.

According to Einstein, the faster we go, the slower time passes. Is that making time go faster? Hardly. Einstein's theory covers physical travel and the speed of light, not the speed of life.

Theories abound about the reason for the sense that time passes faster now than in our youth. Here are some:

A year is a smaller part of our life as we grow older. At age five, a year is 20 percent of our life. At age 50, it is only 2 percent.

We easily forget repeated tasks and daily chores. They merge into a blur, and our memory of past time shrinks.

We are less eager for the future. When we are young, we look forward eagerly to the next significant event—a driver's license, marriage, a first child. Time seems to move faster now because we are not impatiently waiting for the future to arrive.

(Shift your minds into high gear because this one is complex.) Duke University Professor Adrian Bejan concluded our sense of time is related to the number of mental images our brain meets and the state of our brains as we age.

As we get older, we see fewer mental images per second because of changes in vision and less-clear brain pathways for transmitting information. So, when we are very young, our brains process more images per second than when we are older. Process many images; time seems to move slowly. Process fewer images; time seems to move faster.

It's as if our brain has a metronome that provides our sensation of how much time has passed. Ask children to time a minute without a clock, and they will estimate it to be about 40 seconds. Adults will likely guess a minute has passed after 60-70 seconds.

There is an interesting variation on our sense of the speed of time, in addition to it seeming to speed up as we grow older. Time does seem to fly by during novel activities. But when we remember the activity later on, it will seem to have lasted longer than our more mundane experiences. In the memory of a roller coaster ride, for example, we think of it as lasting much longer than the brief 112 seconds of the average roller coaster ride.

Why? Our brains encode new experiences, but not familiar ones. Our judgment of elapsed time is based on the number of new memories created over a certain period.

This new-experiences concept adds yet another theory to the shortening of time as we grow older. If we have fewer new experiences, time seems to shrink.

The moral of the story: to slow down time, find ourselves some new experiences.

Now, if someone could just explain another mystery to me—why my memories of childhood are crystal clear, my memories of the middle years are a little fuzzy, and I can't remember a thing about yesterday's lunch.

9 Is Age Just a Number?

The remainder of my days, I shall rather decline, in sense, spirit, and activity. My season for acquiring knowledge is past. —John Adams at age 35

"Put out that light in center field!" yelled someone sitting on the bleachers ahead of me at a community league softball game. The crowd around him laughed.

I didn't.

The light he yelled about was the shiny top of my dad's bald head. He was playing center field.

I wanted to crawl under the bleachers and hide. "Dad needs to act his age. He is much too old to be playing softball," I thought. "He should be back home in an easy chair."

I was 12. Dad was 35.

Now, at more than double that age, I see 35 as young.

At 50 Dad took up snow skiing, and kept at it until he reached 80. "You are as old as you feel," he said. Now an adult myself, I took pride in his accomplishment.

He often cited Mrs. W. as an object lesson in how not to age. At 60, Mrs. W. decided she was old and should spend her days at home. She stopped attending worship services, and she asked her children to get her groceries for her.

When Dad recited the story, he concluded with astonishment each time, "She lived to 90. She wasted 30 years as a shut-in. Thirty years. Can you imagine?"

I'm not sure my father was right about being as old as you feel. For some of us, being older imposes limitations, no matter how old we feel. Some of my peers now struggle with arthritis or are limited by malfunctioning hearts. Feeling is one component of aging. We all carry an inner child within us, but we can't always follow that child's feelings.

Limits are not solely for the old, however. Decades ago, I received a magazine assignment to write an article about Joel, a preschooler who had lost the use of his arms and legs in an auto accident. I entered his home, prepared to pity him. I found him playing with toy cars, zooming them around on the table with a mouth stick. When he zoomed them off the table, his mother chuckled, caught them, and put them back. (He eventually learned to type with that mouth stick, as well.) I came prepared with pity, and left amazed by coping and hope.

Joel, at five, was a role model for us at the other end of life. He and his mother focused on "can" instead of "can't."

Recently I read an article in which an older adult said, "Age is just a number." Just as I disagreed with my father, I disagreed with her. "It is not just a number," I thought. "The older we get, the poorer our health."

Then I did some research. Over and over again I ran across descriptions of the vast variety in how people age: variety in health, variety in level of independence, variety in employability, etc.

"No two people age at the exact same rate or manner," said the Federal Drug Administration (FDA).

The World Health Organization maintained, "There is no 'typical' older person."

One medical article recommended that physicians classify their patients not just by their age, but also by their stage of health, with Stage A having "independence and minimal chronic illness burden," and Stage D having "disability and dependence on support of caregivers."

I thought of the variety in my peers. Some of my peers played pickleball; others walked with canes. Some took no prescription medications; others took them by the fistful.

The FDA added, "The rate of aging may be influenced by genetics, lifestyle, diseases as well as environmental and socioeconomic factors."

"Hmm," I thought, "I have no control over my genetics, but I can control my lifestyle. I'll need to research that." But that's a topic for another chapter!

When my father was 90 and we waited in a concessions-stand line at Orange City, Iowa's annual Tulip Festival, Dad sat in a chair while the rest of us stood. "I'm getting old," he said. It was the first time I heard him use the O word to describe himself. None of us knew it then, but he already had the lung cancer that would take his life before the year ended. He finally felt his age. He began to enter Stage D of his life.

But, different from Mrs. W., he had lived nearly 30 full and fruitful years.

I will not be skiing at 80. Osteopenia (porous bones) makes it high risk for me. But I would like to follow my father's example, living life as fully as I can for as long as I can.

10 Better with Age

For age is an opportunity no less
Than youth itself, though in another dress,
And as the evening twilight fades away
The sky is filled with stars, invisible by day.
  —*Henry Wadsworth Longfellow*

When I was in my 40s, a retired woman surprised me by saying, "This is a good stage of life, if you have your health." I had pictured retirement years as dominated by chronic illness, slower functioning, and memory loss. My opinion was predictable in a culture which prizes youth. Our society conditions us to look at the negatives instead of the positives of our later years.

Laura Carstensen, director of the Stanford Center on Longevity, sees the positive side: "Though there are problems with old age, and the last year or so of life is pretty bleak for many people, that bleakness characterizes the end of life, not old age per se." She says there are two competing voices on aging: the doom sayers and the romanticists.

I don't want to be a romanticist. Aging has definite drawbacks. As Golda Meier said, "Being seventy is not a sin. It's not a joke either." I know old age is not for sissies, but for today, we are going to look on the bright side.

Duke University's Peter Uble asked groups of 30-year-olds and 70-year-olds which of their two age groups they considered happier. Both groups selected the 30-year-olds. But then, both groups completed a survey on their own happiness. Surprisingly, the 70-year-olds were happier than the 30-year-olds. Older people have proved happier in other studies as well. Although, we live with the stereotype of grumpy oldsters, the data documents the opposite.

Older people have higher levels of positive emotions and lower levels of negative emotions—less sadness, anger, and fear. They also experience less clinical depression and have a lower rate of suicide.

The higher happiness level for older people has multiple dimensions. We maintain a positive outlook and agonize less over petty details. We let go of negative feelings. We have fewer stressors because most major life decisions—education, marriage, career, and family, and job changes—are behind us.

We also worry less about what others think of us. We are comfortable in our own skin, and we have more self-confidence. We even dare to be silly. If we watch any grandparent with a toddler, we become totally convinced of our peers' silliness capacity!

Because we are more emotionally stable later in life, we make wiser decisions than we did earlier. We are less impulsive, we understand what's important, and we consider the long-term impact of a choice.

Having experienced the inevitable peaks and valleys of life, we have learned acceptance, compassion, and empathy. Rather than judging, we imagine what it is like to walk in another's shoes. We accept who and what they are. We also become more accepting of the mystery of life, and of death.

The types of experiences that make us happy are different for the young than for the old. Young people seek thrills—extraordinary experiences. Older adults value ordinary experiences, the momentary pleasures that come to us each day. They are more mindful. And mindfulness—paying attention to the present moment—can help reduce stress and promote good mental health, according to Flinders University researchers.

There's another benefit of longer life. We have accumulated a rich storehouse of stories, and we have gotten better at telling them.

Looking back over the past decade, I realize that ever since I found my retirement niche, I have been more satisfied than in previous decades. But I didn't realize until I read the studies that my higher life satisfaction was typical. I maintained the grumpy-oldster stereotype and considered myself a lucky exception.

It took ten hours of study to convince me that what my retired friend told me decades ago about her stage of life was not just true of her and me, but true in general for many older adults throughout the country.

We have learned to be happy in spite of, instead of because of. We have, for the most part, been granted the request of the Serenity prayer attributed to Reinhold Niebuhr. We have been granted the serenity to accept the things we cannot change, the power to change the things we can, and the wisdom to know the difference.

11 A Purpose in Life

I don't want to achieve immortality through my work. I want to achieve it through not dying. —Woody Allen

Over zucchini bread and coffee, I chatted with two women at a Pella, Iowa, senior-living facility. I asked them about their adjustment to their current living arrangement.

"I just wish I could volunteer somewhere," said Emma wistfully.

Kathleen grew suddenly pensive. "I do too," she said.

"We don't have cars, so it is hard to go anywhere," explained Emma.

A few minutes earlier, Kathleen had been animated as she talked of her first retirement volunteer work. She had tutored first-graders experiencing difficulty learning to read.

I thought, *Emma and Kathleen feel a lack of purpose. They want to feel useful.* I had just been reading about aging and the need for a sense of purpose in life.

A sense of purpose is not simply a specific end goal. It includes our ongoing impact on the world. It is the "why" of our lives.

Earlier in life we often find purpose in our occupations and in raising our children. Later in life we become empty nesters, and often we have retired.

Our earlier purpose in life maybe faded or disappeared. Loss of a sense of purpose is associated with poorer health. One four-year study of older adults revealed that those without a sense of purpose were almost twice as likely to die during the course of that study.

Study after study reveals many positive associations with a sense of purpose later in life. Some studies have shown that a sense of purpose is associated with keeping our brains active and preventing memory loss. A sense of purpose in life also lowers our risk of developing heart disease; it lowers our level of physical disabilities and depression.

Unfortunately, no magic potion or program offers us a ready-made purpose in life. We can't just sit down, invent one, and solve the problem. Purpose in life develops gradually over time.

Finding a sense of purpose can begin by asking what gives us joy. Purpose can be found in the place where what we love meets what the world needs. That purpose isn't necessarily huge. Each of us lives in just one tiny corner of the universe.

Psychiatrist Viktor Frankl offered helpful ideas about developing a sense of purpose in life. Frankl believed each of us possesses a healthy core that can find purpose and meaning. We discover that core through activity and interaction, not through just sitting and thinking about our purpose.

Frankl said we can discover meaning by redirecting our attention from ourselves to others. We can teach Sunday school or lead a scout troop. We can help with crafts at vacation Bible school. We can provide a meal for someone recovering from surgery. Religious beliefs, too, can offer meaning to life.

Frankl said we can also discover the meaning of our lives through what we create. We can write letters to the editor. We can take up knitting or painting or woodworking. At 80, my mother-in-law began to cover wire hangers with yarn and gift them to friends and family.

We can also discover meaning through our experiences and connections. We can take a dance class, watch a documentary, or travel. We can study a new language. We can build new friendships or spend more time with current friends. We can speak with grandchildren in person or on Zoom.

Finally, we can find meaning through our attitude toward suffering. As Frankl suffered in concentration camps during World War II, he could control just one item in his life: his attitude. His captors could not take away his ability to suffer with both grace and courage. When life brings suffering, we can find meaning in maintaining an attitude of gratitude.

Over coffee that day, the wistful longing of Emma and Katharine touched my heart. I wondered what I could do. That afternoon I asked a volunteer coordinator at a local thrift store about options for the two women.

"They could volunteer here, and we could find work to match their abilities," she said. "The public transportation van regularly stops both here and at their residence."

The next morning, I stopped at their apartments, told them about the option, and provided them with the phone numbers they needed. "It might not be exciting work, but it would be useful," I told them.

I don't know if they have taken advantage of the volunteer opportunity.

I do know that making an investigation on their behalf offered a new step in my journey toward experiencing my own purpose in life.

12 A Sound Mind in a Sound Body

To keep the body in good health is a duty; otherwise, we shall not be able to keep our mind strong and clear.
—Buddha

The last time I visited my 95-year-old mother before she died, I took two of my grandchildren along. She beamed when she saw them. "What are your names?" she asked.

Caleb and Phillip, they told her.

"And how old are you?" she asked.

Five and nine.

"I'm glad to see you," she said. "What are your names, and how old are you?"

She asked the same two questions eleven times in our half-hour visit. Then we asked her to play "Jesus Loves Me," on the piano. She obliged, and the boys sang along.

My mother suffered from Alzheimer's. Her short-term memory had shrunk almost to zero. But she could still play the piano.

Like most older adults, I fear developing dementia. Yesterday I researched whether Alzheimer's is hereditary. Some of the early onset Alzheimer's has a genetic component, but late-onset Alzheimer's, like my mother's, does not appear to be transmitted to the next generation.

I was relieved, but during that research I also learned we can strengthen our minds and memories by our lifestyle choices. After a day of following up, I had overloaded my brain with the choices that could improve or maintain my brain health. Our physical, mental, and social activities all can impact our brains. (In this chapter I have only space for physical activities. Mental and social activities will follow in the next two chapters.)

Our brains benefit if we get regular exercise. Aerobic exercise increases the blood flow within our brain. The brain needs oxygen and nutrients, so better cardiovascular health is linked to better brain health.

In a study of one group of women, regular exercise was associated a 9.5 year later onset of Alzheimer's compared to the group that did not exercise. Most experts recommend 30 minutes of moderate exercise five days per week. But they say even 15 minutes of exercise three times per week is better than nothing.

Exercises to maintain balance are also good. Better balance can help reduce the risk of falling and injuring our bodies or brains.

A healthy diet makes a contribution to brain health. The Mediterranean Diet combined with the DASH diet seems to have the most positive impact on our minds. The Mediterranean Diet includes eating lots of fruits, vegetables, legumes, nuts, cereals, and olive oil. It avoids saturated fat, red meat, salt, sugar, and processed foods. The DASH diet is similar to the Mediterranean diet, except it also includes low-fat dairy products, fish, and poultry.

Drinking enough water is also important. As we age, our sensation of thirst declines, making us more vulnerable to dehydration—which can reduce cognitive function. We should drink six to eight glasses of liquid per day. Since our thirst shrinks as we age, we are wise to drink water even when we are not thirsty.

Drinking alcohol as part of our liquid intake, however, is questionable. Alcohol tends to affect us more as we age. US Dietary Guidelines say the maximum alcoholic drinks per day should be one for women and two for men. And maximum recommended tobacco use is, of course, zero.

Maintaining a healthy weight is also wise. Studies have shown that obese people experience faster cognitive decline than people with an ideal weight. The recommended weight for a 5-foot person is 100-120 pounds. For someone 5 feet 6 inches tall, it is 120-150 pounds. For someone 6 feet tall, it is 140-180 pounds. (For the recommended weight for your exact height, you can google "BMI Chart.")

Getting the right amount of sleep, around seven to nine hours, is good for our minds as well. Lack of sleep can lead to difficulty remembering and concentrating, along with an increased risk of dementia. While the results of lack of sleep have long been known, sleeping too much has recently been shown to be associated with lower cognitive and reasoning ability. According to the studies, too much sleep is also associated with increased dementia risk.

An annual routine health screening from our health care provider is also wise. Our provider can screen for diabetes, high blood pressure, high cholesterol, and depression. All of these have a negative long-term impact on how well our minds work as we age. If we are diagnosed with one of these conditions, we should manage that condition well, as recommended by our health care provider, to prevent unnecessary damage to our bodies and brains.

That's a boatload of information and choices. This morning, as I put together these options, I felt overwhelmed.

While I was still at my computer, a friend telephoned, asking me to play pickleball in 15 minutes. I said yes. For lunch I chose peanut butter instead of ham for my sandwich—and I added a lettuce salad and fresh green beans.

I am feeling less overwhelmed. Maybe I just need to make small changes, one choice at a time.

13 Brain Workouts

The brain is like a muscle. When it is in use, we feel very good. Understanding is joyous. —Carl Sagan

I was studying brain workouts when my phone rang. A friend whom I planned to meet later for coffee said, "I can't remember if you are picking me up or if we are meeting at the restaurant. Oh, my memory . . . " Her voice trailed off in frustration.

"We planned to meet at the restaurant," I answered.

I returned to my research. The first quality I found associated with brain health was this: People who cherish and are open to new experiences tend to have lower dementia rates. Locking ourselves into a familiar comfort zone leads to brain mush. So, travel or watching a travel documentary is good for us. So is going to live theater or a concert.

Hmm. I thought I watched those Rick Steves travel documentaries just for fun. I thought the same of that recent trip to an Iowa state park.

Almost all of my reading indicated that a principle for physical health is also true for brain health: Use it or lose it. By challenging our brains, we build up a cognitive reserve. Even if we enter the beginning stages of Alzheimer's, we have extra neurons and neuron pathways to offset the losses.

Learning a new skill is one productive brain

exercise. Taking up knitting, pottery, painting, or woodworking can train our brain cells to fire in new ways. Learning a new computer program or a new language can do the same.

Wow! I took up quilling because I loved the beauty of the paper designs. And I learned basic Spanish because I wanted to communicate with Nicaraguans during mission trips. I didn't realize I was doing my brain a favor.

Playing games in short stints is a good brain workout. Crossword, Sudoku, and Word Find puzzles are good options for solo games. Scrabble and card games are good multiple-person choices. Online card games and Words with Friends make good choices as multi-person brain exercise on the computer.

Hurray! My ritual of a daily game of both Gin and Upwards is good for my mind.

Short-term and long-term memory exercises also provide benefit. How many digits of a phone number can we retain when dialing it? All ten digits? Just six digits and then four? How many items from our grocery list can we place in our shopping cart before we consult that list for items we have forgotten? Can we do a simple math problem in our head without resorting to a pen or a calculator? Can we memorize the lyrics of a song or poem we like? Use it or lose it!

I think I'll challenge my memory the next time I go shopping for groceries. The next time I dial a phone number, I will try to retain all ten digits.

Reading—both nonfiction and fiction—is also good brain exercise. In addition, reading provides us with material for telling stories. And telling stories provides a workout for our memory, our vocabulary, and our organizational skills.

I'm glad to hear that. I enjoy reading—and love telling stories, especially to my grandchildren.

The final brain-training exercise I learned about was meditation. Meditation quiets the brain by focusing on just one item, such as breath or a visual image, and returning to that item whenever our hurry-scurry mind gets distracted by other thoughts.

As I researched, I discovered a study of Mental and Physical (MAP) training funded by the National Institute of Mental Health and the National Science Foundation. The program used 30 minutes of aerobic exercise followed by 30 minutes of meditation. During the meditation, participants concentrated on their breathing, counting their breaths. If their attention wandered, they nonjudgmentally returned their focus to their breathing as often as necessary. (It sounds easy, but it's not. Try it and you will see!) The results of the study were reduction in depression and enhanced synchronized brain activity (which is linked to faster learning).

I already get half an hour of aerobic exercise somewhat regularly. Perhaps I could add meditation afterwards and see how it goes.

My friend and I met for coffee, and her memory functioned just fine. We chatted about our lives. In doing so, we used a third practice for brain health: socializing. Not only do physical and mental activity benefit our minds. Being part of a community does the same. More about that in the next chapter.

14 Sharpened by Community

If we have no peace, it is because we have forgotten that we belong to each other. —Mother Teresa

The loneliest year of my life was the year after I graduated from college. I taught high school 500 miles from northwest Iowa where I had both grown up and attended college. I had a new job, new city, new colleagues, new roommates, and new church. I missed my campus, college activities, and classmates. My new acquaintances were friendly, but I was lonely even when surrounded by them.

Retirement was an easier adjustment for me. I had the same town, same friends, and same church. But retirement adjustment is not smooth for everyone. Some miss their work colleagues. Others move to a new location. And as the years go by, the reasons for loneliness increase. Children might move away. Friends and acquaintances might die. We might be unable to participate in the same activities we once enjoyed.

Long-term social isolation can raise our dementia risk by 64 percent. It can also result in poorer sleep, elevated blood pressure, and a higher cortisol level: all three of these have negative effects on our minds.

An AARP study revealed that Medicare spends $134 more per month on every lonely older adult than for every socially connected one.

What can we do to combat loneliness? We can challenge it on three levels: by changing our thoughts, our feelings, and our actions.

We can challenge our negative thoughts—our self-talk. For example, when we are convinced that our children no longer love us, we can remind ourselves that they have busy careers and families.

We change how we feel. We can take a walk or a warm bubble bath. We can play soothing or energetic music.

Finally, we can change our actions, finding ways to connect with family, friends, acquaintances, and people we do not yet know.

We do well, when seeking to socialize, to ask ourselves what kinds of relationships are important for us. For some people, brief contacts—a friendly exchange with a grocery store clerk or a brief chat with a neighbor at the mailbox—are nourishing. For others, collaborating as part of a volunteer assignment provides the kind of contact they want. Still others treasure deep relationships with their relatives of all ages.

Family relationships can be deepened by familiar activities such as cooking together or by trying new activities such as cooperating on photo albums or scrap books. My husband and I have created a new tradition for our grandchildren. When they are nine years old, they get to spend a week alone with us and we pack that week with as many interesting activities as we can. We also have a family reunion at an out-of-state location every year or two.

People gather at churches, at senior centers, for special-interest clubs, and for card groups such as bridge or canasta. Some people play in a city band. Our Pella city band has members ranging from adolescents to people in their 70s and 80s.

If in-person contact is not possible, we can use technology to help us out. The COVID pandemic helped many of us master those skills. We can use our smartphones to both hear and see one another. Or we can use a program like Zoom or Google Meet to keep in touch with friends and family.

We can invite people to share a meal in our home, or we can go out to restaurant to eat together.

People aren't the only possible companions. Pets can also fill a lonely heart with love and warmth. (Be warned, though, that pets are not only good companions; they also require a commitment and work.)

One very practical step can help some people socialize: If you ever find yourself having difficulty hearing, get your hearing tested. And if you have hearing aids, wear them. I got hearing aids at age 48, when my husband could hear the phone ring from outside of our home, and I couldn't. Now he gets tired of repeating himself when I am not wearing them first thing in the morning.

The same year I got my hearing aids, my siblings and I gave a pair to each of our parents as a 50th anniversary gift. I noticed immediate improvement in their ability to converse in groups.

A final note: you can be socially isolated without feeling lonely, and it is still bad for your health. Studies showed that, even if a person doesn't feel lonely but has few social contacts, that person is at increased risk of depression. This is especially important information for us introverts. I could be happy for a long time reading my books and working with words. But it would not be good for me.

In three chapters, we have now covered the three components of nurturing our minds: physical care, brain workouts, and socializing. Often a single activity meets two of these criteria at the same time. When we join a chess club, we give our minds a workout and we spend time with others. When we volunteer, we often learn a new skill and meet new people. When I go for a walk with my friend, I meet a social need and get physical activity at the same time. (And if it is a Spanish-speaking friend, my brain gets a workout too.)

Over the past three weeks, I've been inspired to try some new activities. I hope you have, too.

Now I'm ready for something lighter. In the next chapter, we'll go to the movies.

15 Movies for Seniors

If you want a happy ending, that depends, of course, on where you stop your story. —Orson Welles

When I google "movies for older adults," *Belfast* pops up as one of AARP's movies for grownups. I research further and learn that this 2021 movie has won multiple awards, including an Oscar for best screenplay.

Among the words critics use to describe it are sweet, neat, light, vivid, soulful, feel-good, rosy, and cozy.

Just the thing for a Friday night date with my husband, I think.

We locate it on Amazon Prime and settle in. We are ready for a pleasant 97 minutes enjoying a movie based on Kenneth Branagh's memories of his life as a boy in Belfast during The Troubles in Northern Ireland in 1969.

We turn on subtitles to help us understand the Irish brogue.

First-time actor Jude Hill as nine-year-old Buddy is a delight. So is Judith Dench as his grandmother. Her grief, at several points in the movie, is stoic and unforgettable. We see the events through Buddy's eyes, so the movie is more about the moments of violence and chaos he experiences than about the larger political issues of the time.

Fifteen minutes in, my husband turns to me and asks in disbelief, "Are you really thinking of this as a movie for older people?"

With its Irish accents, black-and-white photography, and rapidly shifting scenes, the movie is hard work to watch.

"I don't know yet," I answer him, and I turn back to the screen. But I already have my doubts. Will my peers really want to watch a movie that is this much work?

Half an hour later my husband dozes off for a few minutes.

Billy, a Protestant, lives in a neighborhood of both Protestants and Catholics. During riots, the homes of some of his Catholic neighbors are attacked and damaged.

He has a crush on his classmate Katherine, a Catholic. He works hard to get good enough test scores to earn a desk next to hers. Their relationship is indeed sweet, cozy, and rosy. So is his relationship with his grandfather, who gives him advice on his love life.

But the rest of the movie feels jerky and fragmented. I struggle with understanding the Irish accents, trying to read the subtitles fast enough to keep up.

Life in Belfast becomes unsafe for Buddy's family. They struggle with the decision of whether to stay in Belfast or move—to England or even perhaps to Australia or Canada. That struggle provides the central tension of the movie.

It closes with these words of dedication on the screen:

"For the ones who stayed.
For the ones who left.
And for all the ones who were lost."

Those words point to the core of the movie—an empathy for people who have been displaced from the location that they have called home for generations, especially the people of Northern Ireland.

As the closing dedication plays on the screen, I wonder whether I should recommend this movie. It has enlarged my world and my heart. For 97 minutes, I have identified with a family struggling with decisions amid violence erupting in their neighborhood. I have seen that world through the eyes of a child. I have delighted in the work of Jude Hill and Judi Dench. But the movie was not an easy watch. It was not the feel-good movie I expected.

That said, I guess I will leave it for readers to decide whether it is the movie for them.

If readers are looking for a light-hearted, feel-good movie, *Queen Bees*, which I watched a day earlier on Amazon Prime, might be a match.

It is also a 2021 movie and just four minutes longer than *Belfast*. It stars Ellen Burstyn as Helen Wilson, a fiercely independent widow who resists moving to a senior living center until a kitchen fire forces her to live there temporarily while her home is being repaired. The movie was inspired by the producer's own grandmother finding a second chance at love after moving to a retirement community.

Helen encounters high-school-like cliques and power struggles, with one difference. Resident Sally tells her, "In high school we graduate. Here we die."

Queen Bees touches on aging topics (illness, loss of loved ones, loss of independence) with a light touch. As one critic said, "It is lightweight but likable." The plot is predictable, but the acting of a veteran cast saves it from being a total Hallmark movie.

Queen Bees is many of those words used to describe *Belfast*: sweet, neat, light, vivid, feel-good, rosy, and cozy.

But, in this case, those words are true.

16 Words from the Old Days

Slang is a language that rolls up its sleeves, spits on its hands, and goes to work. —Carl Sandburg

This morning I read that my language is outdated if I use the term "mobile phone" instead of "smartphone."

Really! I thought. *Mobile phones were invented yesterday. How can that term be out of date already?*

OK, OK, I realize mobile phones were becoming popular already in the early 2000s, but it seems like yesterday.

Let me tell you about truly old words, ones that come from my youth and early adulthood, before the dawn of cell phones or smartphones. But I assure you, not before the appearance of the triceratops.

If you are under 40, you may not understand the paragraphs that follow. If you are over 60, you may wonder if those paragraphs include any old words at all.

In junior high, I watched a film about the airline industry and the glamorous **stewardesses**. I longed to be one. I thought it was a **humdinger** of an occupation. But at thirteen I already exceeded the 5-foot 10-inch, maximum-allowed height. I was **bummed**. Now airlines accept applicants up to 6 feet 2 inches tall, but it's too late. I no longer think it is a

cool job. And, oh yes, the current term is "flight attendant."

Speaking of **cool,** I know a whole **passel** of outdated words that are variations of it. **Far-out** meant strange-cool. **Funky** meant eccentric-cool. **Groovy** meant modern-cool. **Nifty** meant clever-cool. And **out of sight** meant impressive-cool. That's an out-of-sight list, isn't it?

We had special words for how we felt, too. If something was a **bummer,** it made us sad. If we **dug it**, we understood something. And if we could **hang loose**, we weren't worried at all.

If something was **a gas**, it was very funny. If life was going well, it was **copacetic**. If we were excited about an event, we were **stoked**. If we were frightened about it, we would **freak out**.

If I was surprised by something, I sometimes said, "**Jeepers creepers**!" But never when my mother was nearby. She would have scolded me for swearing.

We had special words to describe people. A sexy woman was **foxy**. A scoundrel was a **rat fink**. A **space cadet** was empty-headed. A police officer was **the fuzz**. We called a divorced woman a **divorcee,** a word I rarely hear these days.

We were proud of our homes, which we called our **pads**. If our homes were in style, we had **wall-to-wall carpets**. And if we were really in style, they were **shag** carpets, with strands of pile long enough to hide a small dog. No one dreamed that the carpet would someday be torn up to return to the original wood flooring—and dozens of long-lost dogs would come tumbling out.

Our stylish refrigerators were **harvest gold** and **avocado green.** We made coffee in a **percolator**, with a wonderful glass bubble in the lid to show the perking. Maxwell House even had a television ad that built an entire tune around the sound of that percolator and called it "Percolabligato."

(If you want to hear it, google "Maxwell House Percolator Ad." You will be convinced you have entered a time machine.)

Popular products like percolators bragged about being sold **coast to coast**. Selling worldwide was the stuff of fairy tales.

If our cars were going fast, we were **bookin' it**. They were equipped with **footfeeds** and **emergency brakes**. When my driver ed teacher called these two items the accelerator and handbrake, I thought he was speaking a foreign language.

In school, if an exam was easy, it was **duck soup**. If it was hard, it was a **bear**. If we thought we did well, we had it **made in the shade**. If we did poorly, we didn't **cut the mustard**. If we did well at academics, but not at sports, we were **eggheads**.

There was no such thing as a training bra. Our mothers only bought us bras when we needed them. And they called them by their full name: **brassieres**. Use the word "brassiere" today, and your son or daughter will ask if you are using a fancy word for a barbecue grill. "It's pronounced 'brazier,'" they will say smugly.

Our church floor was pockmarked with tiny indentations from **high heels**—the term we used for stilettos. At thirteen, I was permitted to get one-inch high heels, the maximum allowed height according to my mother's laws for adolescent footwear.

I teetered around on them for days in practice for my eighth-grade graduation, and I proudly imprinted my share of holes in the square vinyl tiles of the church balcony floor. For eighth grade graduation, all of us dressed our best, in **glad rags.**

Stilettos gave way to **platform shoes** so thick we didn't merely teeter in them—we fell off.

In college, we absorbed the hippie culture, sporting thigh-high **go-go boots** or flowing **peasant dresses.**

We spoke of the power of peace over war as **flower**

power. And we used the words **peace** and **love** as often as we possibly could, both as mantras and on the walls of our dorms.

Come to think of it, those two words have not yet gone out of style, although we do not use them as often as we did back in the 60s and 70s.

Of all the old words, the two I would most like to see return to popularity—and to practice—are those two timeless words: **peace** and **love**.

17 The Child Within

I am still every age I have ever been. —Madeleine L'Engle

It happened to me again last week. Our church bulletin had an announcement about the need for a language arts teacher at an area Christian school. I was intrigued. For ten seconds, I considered applying.

Then sanity returned.

I wondered, "What on earth are you thinking? You are 74 years old, and you left teaching decades ago because you didn't want the unpredictability and stress of managing a classroom!"

Why did I consider the position? Because in those ten seconds the college senior, still alive and well inside of me, took charge. I was an education major in search of a teaching job.

A similar thing happens when I hold an infant in my arms. I think, "How sweet! It would be so nice. . . ."

I am a newlywed again, daydreaming about having that first, perfect baby. This madness lasts only two seconds. Then I remember the sleepless nights, colicky evenings, and fever-filled days. I suddenly recover contentment with grandparenting.

When I take my grandchildren to the playground and use the swing myself, I am six again, thrilling to that weightless feeling at the peak of the arc.

Five years after my son Matt died, I looked at the last picture that was taken of him, and suddenly I was back in time five years, first numb and then mourning his loss.

We carry inside of us each of our younger selves. Morrie Schwartz, a terminally ill professor in Mitch Albom's book *Tuesdays with Morrie*, said, "The truth is, part of me is every age. I'm a three-year-old, I'm a five-year-old, I'm a thirty-seven-year-old, I'm a fifty-year-old. I've been through all of them, and I know what it's like. I delight in being a child when it's appropriate to be a child. I delight in being a wise old man when it's appropriate to be a wise old man. Think of all I can be! I am every age, up to my own."

And that is one of the beauties of being an older adult. When we are young, we do not carry around with us the older ages we will become. But we do carry with us the ages we have been.

Sometimes reliving those stages is pleasant, and sometimes it is not. In *Gates of Excellence*, Katherine Paterson remembers the pain of being a peculiar missionary child, "When I walk into a room full of well-dressed people, I never walk in alone. With me is a nine-year-old who knows her clothes are out of a missionary barrel, her accent is foreign, and her mannerism peculiar—a child who knows that if she is lucky, she will be ignored and if unlucky she will be sneered at. But the gift of maturity is this—not that I can ever excise that frightened, lonely nine-year-old or that I even want to, but that when I walk into that room, I quickly recognize a hundred children just as fearful and desperate as I. And even if they are afraid to reach out to me, I can feel, along with my own nine-year-old loneliness, a kind of compassion, and make an attempt to reach out to them."

You are right, Katherine, I think. *I, too, remember sneers about my appearance as a bean-pole nine-year-old with a mouth too small for her teeth. Thanks for the reminder. I hope that, like you, I can transform the humiliation of those sneers into compassion.*

Writer Madeleine L'Engle wants to preserve those stages of life within her. She says, "This does not mean that I ought to be trapped or enclosed in any of these ages . . . the delayed adolescent, the childish adult, but that they are in me to be drawn on; to forget is a form of suicide. . . . Far too many people misunderstand what 'putting away childish things' means, and think that forgetting what it is like to think and feel and touch and smell and taste and see and hear like a three-year-old or a thirteen-year-old or a twenty-three-year-old means being grownup."

She concludes, "If I can retain a child's awareness and joy, and 'be' fifty-one, then I will really learn what it means to be grownup."

I agree with you, Madeleine. I don't ever want to lose those younger people within me either. Neither do I long to return to those stages of life.

To paraphrase St. Paul, "Day by day I am learning in whatever stage I am, to be content."

18 OK, Google

Respect your parents. They passed school without Google.
–Zoltan Mesko, Football Player

Alexa runs my son Chad's home. Her power and obedience amaze me.

When Chad wants the lights on, he simply says, "Alexa, turn on the living room lights." She pleasantly responds, "OK." And the lights come on.

When he wakes up in the morning, he says, "Alexa, turn on the coffeemaker." Again, her gentle voice consents, and the coffeemaker starts.

He tells us if he leaves home and doesn't remember whether he has closed the garage door, he talks to Alexa on his smartphone. "Alexa," he says, "Close the garage door." If the door is open, Alexa closes it.

A computer programmer, my techie son tells me that to accomplish these feats, he needs an Alexa device in his house and on his phone. He also needs a device on each apparatus he wants to manage.

After Chad has wowed us with Alexa, we visit my equally techie younger sister, a retired computer software representative. Alexa doesn't run Kathy's home. Google does. When Kathy needs to time her cooking, she says, "OK, Google. Set timer for 10 minutes." Google obeys.

When she is running out of milk, she says, "OK, Google. Add milk to grocery list." Google obeys.

"That's incredible," I say to her. "Google serves you the way Alexa serves Chad."

Google hears his name and asks me, "How can I help?"

"Oops!" I say.

"Yes," said Kathy. "You must be careful with his name. I just refer to him as 'G' when I don't want to wake him up."

"Doesn't it bother you having a device in your home that hears everything you say?" I ask. "Especially when that device is connected to the internet?"

"You already run the same risk on your phone, and you carry that with you everywhere, don't you?" she responds.

I suppose I do.

"How much would I need to invest to get started using Google like that?" I ask.

"You have Google on your phone, right?" she responds.

"Sure," I say. I already use Google for my calendar and address book. I often ask him to provide information such as word spellings, state capitals, or ages of famous people. But I have never thought of asking him do other work for me.

I am not interested in a smart home. But I am jealous of having a servant to keep lists and set timers for me.

"You wouldn't need to invest any money at all," Kathy says. "Give me your phone."

I hand it over. She pokes around on it for a minute and says, "It's ready to go."

She has downloaded a free "Keep Notes" app and then googled how to link it to the Google software. After she links it, she tells me to try giving some instructions.

I tell Google to add milk to my grocery list. Google

complies.

"Oh dear!" I say. "I don't really want that on my grocery list."

"Then tell him to delete it," says Kathy.

I tell him. He deletes it.

Over the next several weeks, I find Google to be a cooperative servant who keeps my life in order. He keeps multiple lists, and his timers keep me from burning food and missing appointments.

I feel like such a 21st-century woman when I walk through the grocery aisles with a smartphone in my hand instead of a wrinkled piece of paper.

The first time in the grocery store, though, my phone goes to sleep every 30 seconds, and I must wake it up to read the next item.

Back home, I remember how my sister googled for instructions on linking software. I follow her example and google how to set my screen timeout.

My screen now stays awake for half an hour.

Imitating my techie relatives, I'm beginning to feel a wee bit techie myself.

19 Five Kinds of Wealth

The most precious things in life are not those you get for money. —Albert Einstein

"What is your definition of wealth?" is a question wealth management consultant Jerry Foster sometimes asks people. They often respond with financial and material values.

But when he asks them to complete the sentence, "Wealthy is the person who . . ." most people respond with more contemplative and altruistic values. And this response is richer and truer.

Foster was in Pella in September 2022 to help Vermeer Corporation kick off its training series "Equipped for Life." Vermeer created the series for team members approaching retirement. Series coordinators Dale and Mary Andringa graciously allowed me to attend as a writer.

Foster and the Andringas prefer the term "third season of life" over the term "retirement." Foster said, "The word 'retirement' implies that we are finishing something and winding down, when in reality we should see it as refocusing and living into a new beginning."

He added, "We go through different seasons of life, all of which have different challenges and opportunities, but all of which are equally important, stimulating, and satisfying."

In the September seminar, Foster listed five dimensions of wealth:

- Financial capital: your money, assets, and material possessions—your net worth.
- Relational capital: all the people in your life—relatives, friends, and acquaintances
- Physical capital: your health, fitness, and recreation.
- Intellectual capital: your IQ, education, aptitudes, and skills
- Spiritual capital: the place God and your faith fill in your life.

Foster said these are not separate plates we try to keep spinning atop a stick, running frantically from one to the next. They are more like a collection of balls we juggle, focusing one at a time on just the ball that is in our hand.

Foster said we manage wealth in each of these five dimensions throughout our lives. In his book *Small Changes, Big Results*, he says when we make wise choices in responding to both bad and good life experiences, we can accumulate relational, physical, intellectual, and spiritual capital. If we apologize to a spouse or friend for an action of ours that hurt them, we make a deposit in relational capital. If we choose to sacrifice some time and money to achieve an educational degree, we are generating intellectual capital. When we sit at a funeral, if we ask ourselves about our purpose in life and our destiny after death, we can move toward enriching our spiritual capital.

Foster divides life into thirds: foundation (0-25 years of age), framework (25-60), and finish (60-100). He maintains that the third season can be the most enjoyable phase. We have greater control of our time and are under less pressure. We have a full range of life experiences from which to draw.

According to Foster, already in the second season of life, we begin to set a primary trajectory for our third phase. The trajectory options are indifference, indulgence, and influence.

- The path of indifference is our most likely choice if we just let life happen to us, if we simply maintain the status quo.
- The path of indulgence is a conscious choice to live for ourselves instead of for others. Acquiring, owning, and consuming take center stage.
- The path of influence views every life experience as an opportunity to impact people in a positive way.

Foster says each kind of capital can be useful in a life of influence. We can donate money for the betterment of others. We can mentor a struggling young couple in relational skills we have mastered as a couple. Maintaining our health allows us the physical energy to contribute to the well-being of others. Teaching software skills to a fellow older adult shares intellectual capital.

In spiritual capital, the direction of the influence flows both ways. "We approach God to be influenced by him so we may positively influence others."

Foster recommends two guardrails when walking the path of influence:

- "Don't confuse influence with mere busyness." We need to match our choices of activities with our gifts and talents—our capital.
- "Don't try to measure the effectiveness of your influence by comparing yourself to others." The size of your circle of influence is not crucial. It IS crucial to have a positive impact on people whose lives touch yours.

20 Our Youth-Oriented Culture

"Fear of dying is human. Fear of aging is cultural." —Ashton Applewhite, Anti-ageism Activist

"Happy Birthday!" I said to my husband as I hugged him.

"Thanks. You are now married to an old man," he said.

"You're only 75," I said, attempting cheer. "You won't officially be old until you turn 76. And then . . . then I will find a reason that 76 is not yet old either."

I headed for the bedroom and rethought my response.

I turned back and said, "You said that as if being old is a bad thing. It could be a good thing. You are now mature and wise. Why do we look at being old as automatically bad?"

"Because it's not being young," he said, half serious.

I thought about that the rest of the morning.

When I say, "I'm getting old," I don't say it with pride or satisfaction. I usually say it either as a half-joke that I don't quite believe, or I say it with a touch of sadness, mourning a lost youth.

Doing that is accepting our culture's youth-biased values. I value energy over wisdom and speed over steadiness.

In our culture, we try to preserve at least a façade of youth with hair dyes and Botox.

We fail.

We grow old, and feel an undercurrent of sadness. We mourn our lost youth. We don't realize that in doing so, we are products of a culture which has a youth fetish.

Our culture is the ocean we swim in, and we assume all creatures live in this water. We don't realize there are also land-based creatures.

Our culture values both the appearance and the productivity of youth—their work. UCLA professor Jared Diamond says, "If you're no longer working, you've lost the main value that society places on you." He also says we emphasize independence and self-reliance, which can be lost during the aging process.

Not all cultures have negative views of old age:

- Like many Native American tribes, members of Puget Sound's Squaxin Island tribe value the wisdom that comes with age. Children and young adults serve food to the older adults, who always eat first.
- In South Korean culture, traditionally, a huge family party marks a person's 60th birthday, celebrating their passage into old age. A similar event celebrates 70th birthdays. Older adults are treated with gentleness, respect, and reverence.
- In India, older adults are the head of the family. They provide advice on wedding rituals and family conflicts. Their advice is family law. Younger adults typically care for older family members.
- In China, the "Elderly Rights Law" states that children should never neglect or snub elderly people and adult children should visit their parents often. Chinese older adults can sue their children for lack of financial and emotional support. Some have already sued their children

for not visiting them regularly.
- Japan holds a national holiday every year on the third Monday in September to honor older adults. It is a paid holiday in which grandparents receive gifts and share a meal with their families.
- In Greece, the terms "old man" and "old woman" are not negative words. On a trip to Greece, Arianna Huffington discovered that Greeks address abbots as "Geronda" which means "old man." They call abbesses "Gerondissa" or "old woman." Huffington says, "The idea of honoring old age, indeed identifying it with wisdom and closeness to God, is in startling contrast to the way we treat aging in America."

This afternoon our son Mark and his family came to celebrate Marlo's birthday. Marlo provided them with a window to the past.

He shared with them his just-printed, 175-page autobiography, *Looking Back*. Nine-year-old Caleb studied a picture of Marlo's Doodle Bug, the tiny scooter Marlo drove on the family farmyard when he himself was nine. Marlo read to Caleb the story of crashing unharmed into a building while learning to ride the scooter.

Mark looked at photos of the houses in which we lived as he was growing up and asked questions about them. Our daughter-in-law Elizabeth wept as she learned new details of our son Matt's addiction and death.

Mark and Elizabeth left, leaving Caleb to visit us for the coming week. This evening the three of us played card games together.

Psychologist Erik Erikson, who specialized in studying the stages of life, said that in Western culture, our fear of aging keeps us from living fully. He wrote, "Lacking a culturally viable ideal of old age, our civilization does not really harbor a concept of the whole of life."

Erikson is probably right about our culture in general. We may not have a culturally viable ideal of old age. This afternoon and evening, though, Marlo was living old age with pleasure. Our culture may not have a viable ideal of old age, but that can't stop us totally. Defying the cult of youth, we can each find moments and hours to live our stage of life fully and with joy.

21 On Fatigue and Grandchildren

Fatigue is the best pillow. —Benjamin Franklin

Our grandson Caleb, age nine, spent a week with us. His parents requested that he attend an evening Vacation Bible School program at a local church during his visit, and we agreed.

"Great!" Marlo said. "That will give us a break toward the end of the day. We will probably need it."

"Sure!" I said, thinking not of my energy level, but of Caleb's potential boredom. Marlo sometimes had talked about having a lower energy level than in his younger years. I had never said something similar. I hadn't noticed any diminishing energy level.

Caleb did not get bored. At his request, we played Trash and Flinch (his two favorite card games), along with Sorry and croquet. He also requested a couple of visits to the local library. We took day trips to Living History Farms and the Iowa Science Center in Des Moines.

Together, he and Marlo built and flew a kite. They went to a park together. Caleb helped us prune and organize the toy shelves. He and I took the baby toys to a thrift store, then shopped there for replacements.

Marlo and I tag-teamed some of the responsibilities. Marlo rested while I took Caleb shopping. I did the same while they built the kite together. I tried to write during my breaks. I could not string two sentences together.

After an hour of playing Trash, my focus waned, and I made errors in judgment that left me concerned about dementia. After three games of croquet in the hot sun, I suggested going indoors for a snack—not mentioning I wanted to sit and rest. At the library, while Caleb hunted for graphic novels and Garfield books, I sat in an easy chair, telling myself I had lots of unread books on my shelves at home.

The night after croquet in the sun, I slept 11 hours. Marlo took the morning shift.

My frequent fatigue took me by surprise. I wondered if I had some horrible, undiagnosed disease. I decided to google "fatigue and older adults."

I learned as we age, activities become more tiring. The reason: We lose muscle mass and strength. Our muscles also become less flexible. By age 70, many people have lost 30 percent of their muscle mass. Our lack of energy even has an official name—"anergia."

I met myself in this statement by aging expert Helen Dennis: "For some reason, it seems difficult for some of us to admit we are tired." I had experienced episodes of tiredness before Caleb's visit, but had denied their increasing frequency. I had counted lying on the couch using my smartphone as an activity, not resting.

Dennis pointed out fatigue was seen in a positive light in medieval times, as a sign that someone had reached their limit and needed a rest.

After industrialization, with the need for untiring factory workers, fatigue began to carry a stigma. More recently, concerns about mental fatigue surfaced with the need for ongoing alertness in such jobs as piloting and operating radar.

The experts agreed having less energy as we age is a common complaint.

However, ongoing, incessant fatigue that lasts more than a few weeks might have causes other than aging. It might be time to consult with our health care provider. Causes might include
- Medications we are taking,
- Heart or lung problems.
- Anxiety, or depression
- Shortage of key nutrients
- Chronic pain
- Dehydration
- Sleep apnea

Our health care provider can help determine if our fatigue needs medical intervention.

For normal, intermittent fatigue, experts recommend the familiar list of healthy habits.
- Get regular exercise
- Eat a healthy diet, high in vegetables, fruits, and lean protein.
- Avoid too many carbohydrates
- Stay hydrated.
- Reduce stress
- Have a regular sleep routine
- Don't view electronic screens before bedtime.

Caleb left two days ago, and my energy levels have returned to their pre-visit levels. But there is one change. I am willing to admit that my stamina is less than it was 30 or 40 years ago. I hope the lesson lasts.

I may forget.

At the end of Caleb's visit, as he was leaving with his parents, he leaned forward and said through the car window. "Thanks, Grandpa and Grandma. I had a really good time at your house." Then he smiled and waved goodbye.

His words were sufficient payment for every second of fatigue in the previous week.

Those words I will not forget.

22 Retirement Guilt Trip

Retirement is not the end of the road. It is the beginning of an open highway.

"Don't retire. Retirement is a modern invention," declared three books on retirement I recently read. "An unending vacation is not good for you."

I bristled.

I am retired. I am NOT on permanent vacation. I volunteer for several nonprofit organizations in town. I lead a Bible study. I write. I teach ELL (English as a Learned Language).

My retired friends are not lolling around on permanent vacation either. Granted, they do not work 50- or 60-hour weeks, but they do help build a better world.

I do not want to go back to paid work! I rebel against juggling family duties, employment, and church responsibilities. The to-do list that is never done. Going to bed bone-tired at night. The always-too-early alarm.

I think my experience of mid-life pressure is common. Some people in low-paying jobs need to work two jobs to make ends meet. Others in higher paying jobs feel the pressure to work long hours in a company that keeps raising the productivity bar.

Before we retire, we have unbalanced lives. Life is supposed to be a balance of work and play. Not work, work, work. So, I rebel against the suggestion I find gainful employment.

But I do not believe I am on a permanent vacation. I wondered if other retirees see these years as a permanent vacation. I did some research.

I discovered that retirement is indeed a fairly new concept, which became widespread in the United States with the Social Security Act of 1935. In Germany, the first state-sponsored pension program was launched by Chancellor Otto von Bismark in 1883. Before that, in an agriculture-based society, most farmers worked until they were unable to, leaving the more demanding work to their children as the years went by.

As I researched, I uncovered one myth. Several books maintained that in the early years of social security, people would only to live a year or two after they retired. The average life expectancy at birth in 1940 was only 62.9 years. But that average is so low because of high infant death rates. That same year, a 60-year-old could expect to live to age 75. Today the life expectancy at 60 is 83.5 years. That change is an increase, but not as dramatic as the life expectancy of 62.9 years at birth seems to indicate.

I learned that many older adults still do paid work. In 2019 more than 20 percent of adults over 65 were still working for pay or looking for paid work (That percentage is double the number of people over 65 who were still working for pay in 1985.)

I read an AARP survey revealing 42 percent of retired Americans do some sort of volunteer work. A 2020 "Philanthropy News Digest" survey said that number was 58 percent. I found myself skeptical about those numbers. I suspect that those percentages include only volunteer work for organizations. I wondered if the percentages included taking a pot of soup to an ailing neighbor? Or giving a ride to the doctor to someone no longer able to drive? What about babysitting for grandchildren? I suspect that there is a lot of volunteer work going on that was not counted in this survey, but that is intuition, not data. If volunteering is defined broadly, every retiree I know does useful volunteer work.

When I was taking a spiritual-formation class that required I find a mentor, I asked an 86-year-old to fill that role. She answered, "I have been praying for some way to be useful, and here you come with this request." She said yes. She was now doing volunteer work, although she would not have counted that if she were taking a survey.

In my search for data on the number of people who treat retirement as a permanent vacation, I came up empty. But after my research, writers who see retirees as permanent vacationers and advise returning to work irritate me even more.

Perhaps I have a skewed understanding of the word "work." I equate it with being driven and pressured. However, these do seem to be common conditions of paid workers in our country.

Retirement as continuous vacation is certainly an image promoted in ads. But I simply don't know retirees who fill their lives with coffee times and cruises and golf and pickleball, without also making themselves useful

23 The Care and Feeding of Your Soul

"We are taught more how to care for our cars than how to care for our souls." —Kevin Glesener, Chaplain

"How is it with your soul?" Chaplain Kevin Glesener asked a group of Vermeer Corporation employees who were approaching retirement. Glesener was teaching a class "The Care and Feeding of Your Soul" as part of Vermeer's series "Equipped for Life." I was given permission to attend as a writer.

Glesener told the seminar group that he was speaking from a Christian worldview. In their self-introductions, the group members indicated that they all were people of faith as well.

"We cannot have an impactful life with an impoverished soul," said Glesener. "Soul neglect leads to broken relationships, unsatisfied desires, and chronic discontent. Consequently, a healthy soul is crucial to our wellbeing. . . . Soul care centers and roots you."

In a subsequent interview, Glesener explained centering and rooting to me. "We were created in the image of God. Centering and rooting our soul bring us back to our authentic self and purpose. These are unique for each of us—as unique as our fingerprints."

In the seminar, he told the group that soul care is

crucial for finding peace in the third stage of life. Soul care has three parts—getting things settled with God, settled with life, and settled with people.

He urged the group, first of all, to be present and keep current with God. How? "By spending time," he said. He added that there is value to being part of a church. "Being part of a worshiping community keeps open the channel of communication with God. There is value to habit and ritual."

During the interview he added that personal meditation time is also crucial. He and his wife rise early each morning to read the Bible, respond to it, and pray together.

Second, Glesener advised seminar attendees to make adjustments to this new stage of life. Leaving employment is a significant loss, and we need to take time to acknowledge that loss. Our sense of self-worth is tied to what we do. Glesener said he cried when he left the church he had pastored for 15 years. "If you push the grief aside, it will come out in strange ways." Among those ways are irritability, depression, and overreaction.

Retirement parties are an important ritual for bringing a sense of closure and helping us make the transition. Turning down a retirement party is not a wise choice.

Glesener cited the five stages of grief (denial, anger, bargaining, depression, and acceptance) as also relevant to grieving the loss of employment. These do not necessarily occur in orderly sequence; we may bounce around back and forth among them. This later stage of life is a time of other grief as well, including the eventual loss of family members and friends.

Regardless of the loss, it is important to grieve well and to give ourselves permission to experience the multiple feelings that accompany loss.

Third, he advised making time for relationships with others. The third stage of life is your final chance to

strengthen and mend relationships. Citing *The Four Things That Matter Most* by Ira Byock, he recommended using four phrases in mending and building relationships:
- I love you.
- Thank you.
- Forgive me.
- I forgive you.

He said that Byock's book is often recommended reading for hospice patients and their families, but he recommends it highly for retirement reading as well. The four phrases are as important in the third phase of life as they are during a terminal illness.

Glesener distributed a list of 50 ways to nourish your soul. My ten favorites from his list are:
- Sit quietly in a room and pray or meditate (just listen). Listen for the God whisper.
- Breathe! Take deep breaths several times a day. It can be relaxing.
- Take a class in an area you are interested in or want to know more about.
- Take time to call, contact, or visit a loved one. Tell them how much you appreciate them. Bring them a gift.
- Sit outside in a really dark place with very little background light and just look at the stars and the Milky Way.
- Go to an inspiring movie or play.
- Do at least one unselfish, unnoticed act of kindness for a complete stranger.
- Plan your funeral.
- Go on a drive with no plan or destination in mind. See where the car takes you.
- Go through an old photo album or scrapbook and share memories. Tell stories with a spouse, kids, or grandkids.

As he closed the meeting, Glesener encouraged

those approaching retirement to make a plan for soul care. "Ask yourself, 'What would I like to focus on to help my soul flourish in stage three?' Even in retirement it is wise to have a plan and goals—especially for something as important as the care and feeding of our souls."

24 How to Make a Financial Retirement Plan

The question isn't at what age I want to retire, it's at what income. —George Foreman

"As soon as I retire, I need to make all of my investments conservative ones in order to protect my assets." That's a common assumption of people approaching retirement, and Financial Advisor Devin Reimer says this assumption no longer works for most retirees. The reason? Longevity. "Retirees are now living longer," says Reimer. "If they invest only conservatively, their returns will be lower, and they may run out of funds while they are still living." A 65-year-old couple in good health has an 89 percent chance that one of them will live to 85. That couple has a 44 percent chance that one of them will live to 95.

In an October 2022 interview, Reimer, who has been a financial advisor in Marion County for 12 years, provided me with the information that follows.

He advises clients to begin planning for their retirement in detail three to five years before their anticipated retirement date. He and his Registered Investment Advisor, intellicents, recommend clients think of their investments as two separate buckets.

In the first bucket, they should invest the amount of

income they need for the first three years of retirement. The first bucket should contain short-term, conservative investments (cash, certificates of deposit, treasury bonds, and conservative bond funds).

He advises them to invest the remainder of their assets in a second bucket—long-term funds (stocks, equity mutual funds, and exchange traded funds). Those long-term investments are more volatile, carrying a somewhat higher risk, but historically they have also averaged a better rate of return.

How can people approaching retirement know what they will need as an annual income? Reimer says that number is not the same as their current gross income. Gross income has deductions that will not be taken from retirement income—deductions for a 401K investment, Social Security, and other benefits such as a health savings account. Income tax in retirement will also be different. For example, starting in 2023, retirees in Iowa will pay no state tax on any retirement income.

Since deductions will be different following retirement, it is wise to examine your current needs, beginning with your net income. To calculate your gross income needs in retirement, a good rule of thumb for most people is to take your current net income and add 12 percent for taxes.

(That percent is the income tax rate for incomes of $20,551 to $83,550 for a couple. For higher incomes or incomes for a single person, google "income tax brackets," and you will find the current tax brackets for you.)

If your current take-home pay is $48,000 per year ($4,000 per month), you need an annual gross income of $54,545 to match your current standard of living.

Social security will provide some of the gross income you need, and you can learn what your social security payment will be by going to www.ssa.gov, signing up for an account, and looking at your potential income statement.

For the sake of this example, let's estimate your gross income from social security will be $24,000 per year ($2,000 per month).

If you subtract $24,000 per year from the gross income you will need, the remaining amount you need annually from investments is $30,545. When you retire, your short-term investments should total three times this amount—$103,635. (This formula is only an approximation because the amount of taxes you will owe can vary with the type of investment you are withdrawing.)

Having a three-year supply of funds in low-risk, easy-access investments will protect you from needing to withdraw money from long-term investments in conditions like the 2022 market, during which stock values were down.

A financial consultant can help you calculate the chances that your long-term investment portfolio will last as long you live. If it looks as if you may run short, it might be wise to keep working and saving for a few more years. Or you might supplement your income with part-time work. Or you could look for ways to reduce your living expenses.

Approaching retirement is a complex subject, and the information above, which can change from one year to the next, only begins to scratch the surface of the variations, details, and choices.

What's the bottom line? It is wise to begin planning in advance and to consult with a financial expert as you make those plans.

The above is provided for general information purposes only and is not intended to be investment advice. Consult with your financial advisor before making investment and donation decisions.

25 Charitable Use of Individual Retirement Accounts

I have found that among its other benefits, giving liberates the soul of the giver. —Maya Angelou

"If you are at least 70.5 years old and have assets in an Individual Retirement Account (IRA), the smart way to donate to charity is often from that IRA," says Financial Advisor Devin Reimer from the Registered Investment Advisor, intellicents. If you make Qualified Charitable donations (QCDs) directly from your IRA, neither you nor the 501(c)(3) charity receiving the donation will need to pay taxes on those dollars.

In an October 2022 interview, Reimer, who has been a financial advisor in Marion County for the past 12 years, explained to me the benefits of QCDs. What follows is based on that interview.

QCDs have been around since 2006. Reimer said that using QCDs to make charitable donations has become especially valuable after the Tax Reform Act of 2017. That reform act increased the standard income tax deduction and reduced itemized deductions. Effective 2018, the standard deduction went from $13,000 for a married couple to $24,000.

The result: many fewer people now itemize their

deductions—including their charitable donations—to reduce their tax liability. Not itemizing means they now pay income tax on the money they are giving to charities.

Normally, when you withdraw money from an IRA, you pay tax on that withdrawal. But if you have a donation made directly from your IRA to a qualified charity, you are donating pre-tax dollars.

If your income as a couple is between $20,551 and $83,550, your federal tax bracket is 12 percent. If you donate $500 to a charity as a QCD directly from your IRA, the charity receives the full $500. If you first withdraw the $500 from your IRA, you will pay 12 percent tax on it for a total of $60. This will leave you with only $440 to donate to the charity.

If your income as a couple is between $83,550 and $178,150, your tax bracket for that money is 22 percent. Donating $500 directly from your IRA is still $500. But donating it after 22 percent taxes, you would have just $390 left to donate to the charity of your choice.

The ceiling for donating QCDs is quite high: $100,000 per person per year.

Processing a QCD is not difficult. Your chosen charity will know whether it is a 501(c)(3) nonprofit and qualifies for QCDs. If it qualifies, you can provide your investment management company with the name of the charity, its mailing address, and the amount you wish to donate. Some investment management companies send the check directly to the charity. Others provide the checks (made out to the designated charity) for you to mail.

You will receive a 1099 form for your contribution and need to report it on your tax return.

This can be especially valuable when IRA holders reach 72 and are required to take minimum distributions from their IRAs. Instead of taking all or their Required Minimum Distribution (RMD), they can designate some of it to go directly to a charity and reduce their tax burden for the year. With careful calculations and planning, they may even be able to keep their income down in a lower tax bracket.

If people have designated a charity to receive part of their estate, it is good financial planning to designate the charity as beneficiary of the IRA, or a percentage of the IRA. The reason: a charity will not pay income tax on funds from an IRA, but your heirs will pay income tax on any IRA moneys they receive. Heirs will not, however, pay income tax or capital gains tax on post-tax assets such as Roth IRAs and assets purchased with post-tax moneys. (For Roth IRAs, investors pay taxes on the amount they are investing, and then no income tax or capital gains tax is due on any appreciation in value of that asset.)

An estate of a single person in Iowa needs to exceed $12.06 million before any estate tax is due. The estate of a couple needs to exceed $24.12 million in value before any estate tax is due.

The above is provided for general information purposes only and is not intended to be investment advice. Consult with your financial advisor before making investment and donation decisions.

26 Senior Scams

There are so many scams on the internet nowadays. Send me $19.95, and I will tell you how to avoid them.

"Aren't you excited?" the caller asked.

"I would be if I believed you," my husband Marlo said.

Marlo had just been told he had won $2 million in the Publishers Clearing House Sweepstakes. To claim his prize, he needed to meet the representative at the local Walmart parking lot.

Immediately.

Was the call genuine? How could we tell? We didn't want to be swindled, but we didn't want to miss out on $2 million, either.

According to the Senate Special Committee on Aging, swindlers cheat older adults out of $2.9 billion per year. When seniors fall for a scam, they typically lose $500 to $1500. The average loss for younger adults is $300 to $400 per scam.

Why is there so much scamming of older adults? It is a low-risk crime because it is difficult to prosecute. Seniors are less likely to report losing money in a swindle than younger adults, and seniors often have more available cash.

Swindlers can have two different goals. Some seek

our personal and financial information; they want to steal and use our identities. Others simply want our money.

These con artists may contact us on the internet, by the telephone, or in person. They usually present us with something wonderful or something terrible. They may appeal to either our fear or our greed.

Fear frauds vary widely. We are being audited by the IRS. Our deceased relative owed the scammer money. Our supposed grandchild desperately needs cash. Our health insurance may be inadequate. Our computer has a virus.

Greed cons also vary. We can invest in a luxurious retirement development in Central America. An available credit card has no interest payment. We have won a sweepstakes or lottery. A Nigerian prince is looking for a partner to help claim his inheritance. We can have our home reassessed and lower our taxes. We are offered an expensive product at an incredibly low price. A pyramid scheme promises an impressive payback. We can work at home and earn a high hourly wage.

Some scams appeal to our hearts, pretending to be charities in need of funds, especially following a natural disaster. Another appeal to our hearts is an online romance fraud. Romance scams take longer than most scams, but the average payoff is also considerably higher as lonely people repeatedly provide funds for a "soulmate" con artist.

How we can spot a scam:
- If a website or email has grammar or spelling errors, it has a high chance of being a scam.
- If someone asks for your personal or financial information on the phone, hang up. No legitimate government organization or business will telephone you and ask for this type of information. Social Security never contacts people by phone. If someone is trying to sell you

something on the phone, tell them you don't make purchases over the phone. You need the information in writing.
- If someone asks you to pay in an unusual way—by money order or gift card for example—they are very likely trying to defraud you.
- Swindlers pressure their targets to act immediately. They create a sense of urgency, with either a crisis or immediate deadline.

What should we do if a swindler attempts to defraud us? Even if the scam was unsuccessful, you should report it to state and federal authorities.
- In Iowa contact the Iowa Consumer Protection office. Email: consumer@iowa.gov. Phone: 515-281-5926. In other states, google "How to report scams in [name of your state]."
- Contact the federal government's Federal Trade Commission. Online: https://reportfraud.ftc.gov. Phone: 877-382-4357

When Marlo and I received that call that claimed to be from Publishers Clearing House, I had not yet done the above research. We did not know we should report attempted fraud. But we did know enough to check out the offer before acting.

Marlo tentatively agreed to meet the caller at Walmart, as requested. Then, before doing anything else, we googled Publishers Clearing House scams. Neither of us remembered registering for a Publishers Clearing House prize, so we were especially suspicious.

We found the following information: "Does the prize have a high value? PCH doesn't contact winners of prizes worth more than a couple of hundred dollars by email, bulk mail, or telephone. They appear in person or send a certified letter."

Our suspicions were confirmed. We did not drive to the local Walmart parking lot for the requested meeting.

Why did the swindler want us to meet him at

Walmart? What would have been his pitch, had we appeared there? He might have requested our personal information and then presented us with a fake check which would have bounced. He might have said we needed to pay a processing fee for taxes and expenses before we could claim our check.

We will never know.

But we do know this: if an offer appears too good to be true, it probably is.

27 Pangs While Purging

The Greek word for return is "nostos." "Algos" means suffering. So, nostalgia is the suffering caused by an unappeased yearning to return. —Milan Kundera, Writer

"Is it time to get rid of this?" my husband Marlo asks. He shows me a memory display box that has been on a garage shelf since we downsized to a duplex three years ago. I made the memory box decades ago, early in our marriage.

He suggests, "We can take the mementos out and donate the box to a thrift store."

"I suppose," I sigh. "I don't plan to display it anywhere."

Marlo removes the glass from the front of the box, and I pry loose the small mementos.

Two items belong to Marlo: a pocket watch from his grandfather and a high school band medal. Marlo says the band medal can be tossed, but he wants to keep the watch.

The remainder of the items are mine. I start with a miniature landscape made of a lava rock, a piece of sandstone, and a flat shell that has functioned as a mini-moon. I no longer remember where any of these came from, so I can dispose of them. The same holds true for a miniature crocheted basket, a tiny covered wagon, and an inch-tall spray of silk flowers.

After that, disposal gets harder. A glass squirrel tugs at my heart. It is the only thing left from a huge glass terrarium that we owned in the 1970s during the terrarium fad. An Empire State Building and a Statue of Liberty are from my 1968 spring vacation trip to New York City. A charm bracelet sports a dozen high school medals—speech, debate, honor roll, newspaper staff. . . .

I wonder if it still fits me.

It does.

I put it on my wrist and the metals clank with their familiar jangle from the past. Their weight is familiar too.

I remove more items. My track medals are glued into the memory box separately. They did not fit on the charm bracelet. I decide I can part with those. I identified more with academics than athletics.

As I look again at the miniature squirrel and New York buildings, bittersweet nostalgia rises, as it often does when I spend time with treasured mementos from the long-gone past. I decide I can display them on the chest of drawers next to my file cabinet. The squirrel can join the ceramic butterfly already there. The two New York building miniatures can go next to my statue of Peter Stuyvesant.

A marble egg (a gift from a cast of a play I student-directed in college) has discolored over the years. I wonder if it can be made attractive again. I submerge it in bleach water. In the bleach it fades and grows dull. I discard it.

An ornate cross my neighbor created with thin, varnished slices of walnut shells gleams too beautifully to toss. I have several crosses hung above light switches as reminders of Christ. I take a pushpin from the bulletin board above my desk and fasten the cross above my office light switch. Maybe later Marlo can help me hang it from a tiny nail which will be less visible than the pushpin, but this will do for today.

Except for the charm bracelet, the remaining items would just clutter up a drawer. I decide to dispose of them. (Instead of "trashing," I choose to think of it as "disposing." It's a less painful term.)

That leaves the charm bracelet dangling from my wrist. I look at it, and I am a high school student again, proudly walking to the front of the auditorium to receive each one of them.

But that was in another life. I am now long past the time when I take ego satisfaction from high school medals. At least I should be.

Perhaps I can wear it occasionally as a reminder of the fleeting nature of time. It can remind me to be present to the moments as they pass. I place it in my jewelry box.

Sorting these mementos, I wonder whatever happened to the items I removed from another memory box—a printer's drawer—shortly after downsizing to this duplex. I search through several wooden boxes until I find the right one.

As I open it, I remember. When I emptied the printer's drawer I couldn't to part with any mementoes, except for 25 keys to unidentified doors and locks that I had kept in case someday I discovered those keys' purpose. That someday had never come, so I disposed of them. The remaining items I put in this box—my silver baby spoon, a Sunday school pin, a piece of coral from Hawaii . . . until I could face parting with them at a future date.

Is today the date? I consider the ache beneath my ribs and the fluttering in my stomach. I close the box.

Parting may be sweet sorrow, but it remains sorrow, nonetheless. And today I have endured all the sorrowing my heart can handle.

Next week I may have the strength to attack the printer's drawer mementos.

But not today. No, not today.

28 Lighting Small Corners

Where there is no vision, the people perish.
—Proverbs 29:18

As a child in Sunday school, I often sang "This Little Light of Mine." Our teachers led us in an adapted version, not part of Harry Dixon Lowe's original lyrics. We sang about shining that light all over our town, our city, our state, and the whole world.

We sang another song about light, too. It ended with, "In this world of darkness, we must shine. You in your small corner, and I in mine."

I liked the idea of being a big light shining over the whole world. Being a little light in a small corner had no appeal.

I think about my small corner today as I proofread a document. I add and remove commas, correct spellings, capitalize letters, and fix grammatical errors. It is time-consuming work—and, frankly, not very much fun.

I am a reasonably competent proofreader, but I prefer to research a concept, make a discovery, and then discover more about the topic as I structure writing paragraph by paragraph.

Proofreading doesn't seem like very important work. It is so picky; each change is so small. It's a minuscule light in a tiny corner.

When I graduated from college, I believed I would shine my light over great distances. I thought it would be huge. I was sure my classmates and I would change the world.

These days I no longer believe that.

I will never write the great American novel or even a nonfiction bestseller. I will never speak to crowds of thousands. My name will never be recognized across the country.

I write a column for a small newspaper. I lead a five-person Bible study. I volunteer for a few local service organizations. I clean my house, cook meals, go for walks, play pickleball, and attend worship services. In each activity, I occupy just a small corner.

As I have aged, I have made peace with that small corner. I have come to recognize that most people in the world work in small corners.

Some of us deliver a meal to an ailing neighbor. Others of us teach Sunday school or volunteer to tutor an at-risk grade-school student. Some of us work at thrift stores that earn funds to provide free Bibles or raise money to help people who need a hand up in this world. Others of us drive frail, elderly friends to doctors' appointments.

However, lighting our small corners is more than volunteering. A simple smile and greeting to a Walmart clerk while shopping lights a small corner. A cheerful conversation with a nurse helping you dress also lights a small corner. Playing with grandchildren lights a small corner.

A story is told of two bricklayers working side by side. They put down a layer of mortar and embedded straight rows of bricks in it, placing bricks in straight rows day after day. A passerby stopped and asked, "What are you doing?"

"Duh. . ." thought the first bricklayer. "That's obvious."

But he answered anyway. "I am laying bricks."

The second bricklayer had a different answer. He replied with pride, "I am building a cathedral."

Both men did the same job with equal skill. But the second man worked with vision.

I need vision, too.

The document I am proofreading is an application by a Cambodian nonprofit organization for a grant of $20,000. It was written by the agency's Cambodian director, Sovann Neth. English is his second language, and he needs the writing to be more polished when it is received by the granting agency. The grant will help Sovann and his team prevent human trafficking of poor Cambodians who migrate to cities or other countries to find work.

I will choose to look at today's proofreading with vision. Comma by comma, word by word, I will lift my eyes and view Sovann, his team, the granting agency—and our mutual goal of preventing human trafficking. I will see the whole cathedral.

As each of us lights our small corner, that is a lot of light indeed!

29 The Aging of the Boomer Bubble

Well, the big elephant in the whole system is the baby boomer generation that marches through like a herd of elephants. —Senator Lindsey Graham

Born in 1948, I am on the leading edge of the baby boomer bubble. We are so named because of the boom in births after soldiers returned home from World War II. Often our name is shortened to just boomers.

Baby boomers were born between 1946 and 1964, so we range in age from 59 to 77 years in age. There are 71.6 million of us in the United States.

Because of that bubble of boomers and because of lengthening life spans for older adults, an ever-increasing percentage of older people is predicted. In 1950, just 8 percent of the US population was over 65. In 2019, that percentage rose to 16 percent. By 2050, it is projected to rise to 25 percent.

What to name this coming bubble has become controversial. The terms "silver (or gray) tsunami" (and variations such as "age wave" and "gray horde") first appeared in the 1980s in reference to population aging. Around 2010 silver tsunami started becoming the widely accepted shorthand used by demographers, economists, and other writers concerned about aging populations.

Some writers object to the term as ageist and overly

dramatic. A tsunami is not predictable, they say. An aging population can be foreseen and prepared for.

Senior advocate Ashton Applewhite wrote, "The phrase [silver tsunami] summons a frankly terrifying vision of a giant wave of old people looming on the horizon, poised to drain the public coffers, swamp the health care system, and suck the wealth of future generations out to sea."

Writers have suggested kinder names such as "gray bloom," "elderswell," and "eldersurge." Perhaps the term "aging boomer bubble," which I used for this chapter, would work. However, none of these terms have the simplicity and attention-getting drama of "silver tsunami."

Does the tsunami term raise unnecessary fears?

In some areas, it would seem so. Experts have predicted that the aging boomer bubble will cause a glut of houses for sale and significantly depreciate the housing market. They have also predicted that, as boomers retire, there will be a knowledge shortage in business and government. Neither of these predictions shows signs of coming true. Boomers are tending to keep their houses and to age in place. And more of them are extending their working years, so the dearth of knowledge may not be as severe as predicted.

Also predicted was a shortage of specialized housing for seniors. There is currently no shortage of private-pay aging communities or assisted living housing. There are sufficient nursing home beds.

Predictions on what will happen to our national productivity are mixed. Some experts say that with a lower percentage of working adults, our GDP will fall. But a study of European populations that are aging ahead of the US has shown no correlation between an aging population and a drop in productivity.

However, there are some worrying shortages. A staffing shortage is causing nursing homes to limit their admissions. Low-income housing for older adults is already in short supply. One study predicts that the number of homeless people over 65 will triple in the next decade.

Experts have also predicted that as the older population has increasing health care needs, the US health care system will be overwhelmed. A health care shortage remains a significant concern.

Perhaps the tsunami term is overly dramatic and triggers unnecessary fear. On the other hand, perhaps those in power should begin preparing for a further. increase in the senior population. It is time to prepare additional care centers and low-income senior housing. Maybe drama is necessary to spur action.

Sharona Hoffman, author of *Aging with a Plan,* suggests swift government action to adjust to the increase: Make long-term care insurance more accessible; perhaps subsidize it. Improve the working conditions of professional caregivers to combat the worker shortage. Increase affordable public transportation to permit the frail old to have more independence when they lose driver's licenses. Offer incentives to health care professionals to encourage them to practice geriatrics.

A low-cost housing shortage is already upon us. Government could provide financial incentives for contractors to encourage the building of lower-cost homes. It could reduce restrictions on loans for condo purchases, making small condos available for first-time home-buyers. Data show that there are millions of low- and moderate-income people who qualify for a mortgage. We simply need available housing for them.

Instead of debating what term is appropriate, perhaps we can lobby our local, state, and national governments to prepare health care and housing for the coming bubble regardless of whether or not it will resemble a tsunami. We can also stay tuned for further developments as time goes on.

30 On Antiques and Aging

I'm the oldest antique in town. —Norman Rockwell

The pitcher and basin on our dining room hutch look as if they come from the 1800s. Actually, we bought them new in 1975, the first year of our marriage. We didn't really *buy* them, though. In that before-online-registration era, we had received two electric frying pans as wedding gifts. We traded one for the pitcher and basin. We didn't choose it because it looked antique; we chose it because it was pretty. We liked its graceful lines and green stenciling.

A few months later we bought a half-century-old, two-story home at 719 East Rose Street in Owatonna, Minnesota, for $16,000. The day we signed the loan papers I lay awake into the early morning hours, overwhelmed by the mountain of debt we had committed ourselves to. In the ensuing months, I slowly adjusted to that mountain.

Our home's high ceilings, wide trim boards, sheer curtains, and pull-down shades reminded me of my grandmother's house. The house, along with the pitcher and basin, called out for antique furniture. We saw a reader ad for an antique table and sideboard for $350. The ad said it was a pedestal table with claw feet. Both the table and the sideboard were solid oak, stained a walnut color. The table was just like my grandmother's! We went, we saw, we bought. We scrunched it into our van and unloaded it. We positioned the pitcher and basin on the sideboard, and I prepared for pleasure.

It failed to materialize. Seated there, I didn't fondly remember my grandmother. I *became* my grandmother gnarled, stout, and stooped. Sitting at the table, I didn't feel pleasure. Only 28, I felt old.

We've made a terrible mistake, I thought. But I hesitated to tell my new husband. What if he likes the antique furniture? How will we ever resolve this issue? Marlo will think I am fickle. . . . Maybe I will like it better with time.

I didn't.

After a month, I sent out a feeling flag. "I feel a bit old when I sit here," I said, hesitantly.

"Really?" Marlo said, "So do I."

"I don't like the feeling," I said.

"Neither do I," he said

"Maybe I would feel differently if it were an antique in a new home," I reasoned. "But in this house, it just makes me feel old and tired."

"Maybe we will like it better with time," Marlo said.

We didn't.

Eventually, one of us felt old and tired enough to venture, "I wonder if we should sell this set and buy something new instead?"

"I wonder . . ." The other of us responded.

Several conversations later, "I wonder" morphed into "Let's try advertising it for sale."

We decided to price it for a profit of $25. Both of us knew, but did not say, that $25 was poor hourly wages for our time loading, transporting, and unloading the set.

It soon sold, and we replaced it with a new, distressed-pine table and hutch. We added chairs to match. Over the decades, the pine got more distressed with multiple dings, scratches, and gouges from three growing boys. Once the nest was empty, we replaced the dark pine with a light oak set.

Nearly 50 years have passed, and we have acquired only two tiny antiques—a coffee grinder and a clawed-feet piano stool. At a half-century of age, perhaps the pitcher and basin can now be considered antique as well.

But over the decades we never again felt a yen for antique furniture. The pitcher and basin sit on the newish oak hutch.

These days we don't *feel* old; we *are* old. But we still don't want an antique table and sideboard shouting that fact at us every day.

31 Senior Moment Debate

The effect of cultural expectations on recall and performance is powerful. —Anti-ageism Activist Ashton Applewhite

Sometimes when older adults have a momentary memory lapse, they say, "Oops, senior moment." I have said it myself.

I used to think it was a pretty harmless phrase. After all, those memory lapses do occur more often in older adults than in younger ones.

Then I read the research of Yale Psychologist Becca Levy and other aging experts. They say that calling a memory lapse a senior moment may be a self-fulfilling prophecy. If we think of ourselves as forgetful because of our age, we become more forgetful.

Levy and others call this term a form of ageism. According to Levy, "Ageism is the most widespread and socially accepted prejudice today."

In a weekly pickleball gathering of mostly older women, we normally number off and then are assigned partners by numbered pairs. Last week, we were assigned numbers, and the person in charge read off the names of paired partners instead of just the numbers.

"Thanks for reading the names instead of the

numbers," said one member, smiling. "I didn't have to ask you to remind me what my number was!"

"We are starting to need that!" said another. And we chuckled.

I was among those laughing.

Back home, I wondered. Was my laughter about memory lapses also a self-fulfilling prophecy? Does it contribute to my belief in a failing memory? How much does my distrust of my memory affect my memory?

In *Breaking the Age Code*, Levy wrote that she flashed positive words about aging on a screen for one group of older adults and negative words about aging for another group, too briefly for the people to be aware of them. The people exposed to positive messages showed better recall and more confidence than those exposed to negative words.

Levy also tested the cultural perceptions and memory of three different cultural groups: hearing Americans, deaf Americans, and mainland Chinese. The hearing Americans had the most negative perceptions of aging—and they did most poorly on the memory test.

In different tests, she found that older people with positive views of aging compare favorably with those who have negative views:
- They have better handwriting.
- They walk faster.
- They are more likely to fully recover from severe disability.
- They live an average of 7.5 years longer.

How do we challenge and change our negative views of aging? Levy says the first step is awareness. She says to write down the first five words that come to mind when you think of an older person. Do this quickly without rejecting any of the words that come to mind. Don't think. Just list. Make your list before reading further.

According to Levy, an awareness of your bias is the

first step. If the first three or four words in your list were negative, you probably have negative views of aging.

To increase your awareness, she suggests writing down all the portrayals of aging people you see in a week and making a list of their positive and negative traits.

To counter a negative bias, she suggests creating a portfolio of positive models for aging (maybe five or so) and reviewing this list regularly.

In regard to memory glitches, she cautions not to instantly blame forgetting on aging. It may be that you were multitasking. You might have been distracted.

Besides, younger adults have memory lapses too. Starting in their 20s, all adults have memory lapses. Older adults simply have them a little more often.

You can also counter memory lapses by reframing your self-image. Remind yourself of your wisdom moments—when you pass on a bit of information or a thought to a younger person. Reflect on how over the years you have mastered the ropes of different tasks. Think about your uncommon skills, such as the ability to do math problems without a calculator. Relish the empathy and resilience that have come to you over the years. And enjoy each moment of life as it comes to you.

Will I stop using the term "senior moment?" I think I will. I will probably use the term "memory glitch" instead.

I will not deny others their right to use the term. However, when others call their memory lapse a senior moment, I may gently remind them that they have wisdom moments as well.

Were we ageist at the pickleball courts when we laughed about reading our names instead of our numbers? The women who play certainly don't see themselves as decrepit. They are, after all, running around on the court and hitting a ball for two hours.

I think one member of that group had it right when she said, "We can all remember our names!" We laughed at her comment, too, but she had reframed the situation for us. She had given us a positive frame to counterbalance the negative one.

The next week, the person in charge read off just the paired numbers to designate partners. And we all remembered our numbers!

32 The Best Years

Don't worry. These are the worst years of your lives.
—Wendy Lustbader, to a busload of 18- to 24-year-olds.

On average, who is happier, a 30-year-old or a 70-year-old?

In 2006, researchers at the Veterans Administration in Ann Arbor, Michigan, asked two groups of people a pair of questions. The average age of the first group was 31. The average age of the second group was 68. Questions researchers asked were:
- Estimate the average person's happiness at 30 and at 70.
- Estimate your own happiness at your current age.

When evaluating others, both the younger and older group thought that younger people have a greater sense of well-being than older people. But when asked about their own happiness, younger people ranked their own happiness lower than older people did.

The study confirmed two facts:
- Our culture believes older people are less happy than younger people.
- Actually, older people are generally happier than younger people.

Dr. Laura Carstensen and her team of researchers at the Stanford Center on Longevity, who have spent the past 30 years researching aging, found similar results. But Carstensen says happiness is a vague term which can refer either to life satisfaction or a set of emotions.

According to Carstensen, life satisfaction questions are cognitive questions. They call for a deliberative judgment, a measure of one's life. When Carstensen and her team studied happiness as life satisfaction, they found a U-shaped curve. Life satisfaction is high at age 20, declines until roughly age 50, and then rises again through age 80.

Happiness as an emotion can be viewed as both the presence of positive emotions (e.g., excitement, calm, joy) and the absence of negative emotions (e.g., sadness, fear, anger). To study this, Carstensen's team sampled positive and negative emotions of people aged 18 through 94. She found positive emotions remained stable or rose slightly over the decades. But negative emotions declined significantly as people grew older. So, asked about how they felt "on balance," taking both positive and negative emotions into account, happiness increased in a linear pattern, rising from age 18 through age 94.

In a podcast interview with Wes Moss, Carstensen said her team of scientists hardly believed their own results at first. They thought perhaps the results could be explained by masked depression, cognitive decline, or brain atrophy. Further studies revealed none of these theories could be supported by evidence.

Whether life satisfaction or emotions are being measured, older people become happier as the years go by. Some call this the paradox of aging. It is a paradox that despite physical declines of aging, happiness rises.

Carstensen wondered whether older people had the resilience to respond positively to inescapable, prolonged stressors. Might they do worse under these circumstances than younger people? With the advent of COVID-19, Carstensen and her team had the opportunity to study both younger and older people under the prolonged stress of COVID conditions. With social distancing and stay-at-home protocols, COVID created a sort of stress lab. During COVID restrictions, Carstensen's team asked older people and younger people the same emotion questions they had asked in previous studies. Contrary to news stories at the time, they found older people were enduring COVID conditions much better than younger people, even though older people's risk factor was higher than younger people's.

Carstensen and her team think the mechanism for this happiness increase is the shrinking amount of time remaining for aging people. "For older people, the future is more constrained," she explained. "As people run out of time, it becomes more valuable."

She said older people have been relieved of the burden of the future. They are able to live in the moment, to notice the rose, the singing bird, the blue sky. Life feels better.

In a TED Talk, Carstensen listed behaviors of older people that benefit their well-being. They:
- Live in the moment
- Know what's important
- Invest in sure things
- Deepen relationships
- Savor life.

Carstensen's research invigorates me as I face the later years of life. I'm putting her list of beneficial behaviors on my bulletin board. I will read it every day until it is embedded deep within my mind and heart.

33 The Importance of Balance

One's reach should exceed one's grasp, or what's a heaven for? —Adapted from Robert Browning

Eighty-year-old former radio show host Garrison Keillor mentioned in a recent email that he had passed a balance test at Mayo Clinic: He stood on one foot for 10 seconds with his eyes closed.

I tried.
I failed.
I worried.
I began researching fall risk for older adults.
Here is what I learned.

Falls rank second in the general population as a cause of accidental death. In the senior population, falls rank number one. One out of four people 65 and older falls each year. And one out of five of those falls results in serious injury—broken bones or a head injury.

If you have fallen in the past year, your risk of falling in the next year is doubled.

I have fallen in the past year.
I worried even more.

But my research also said balance can be improved. So, I researched balance improvement.

I learned you can improve your balance with simple

exercises. Here are two sample exercises I found at www.healthline.com. The Internet has many more exercises available, at varying levels of difficulty.

Rock the boat
- Stand with your feet hip-distance apart.
- Lift your left foot and bend your knee at a right angle, bringing your heel toward your bottom. Hold this position for 30 seconds.
- Then do the same with your right foot.
- Repeat each side three times.

Heel-to-toe walk (strengthens your legs and improves balance)
- Stand with your heels touching the wall.
- Place your left foot in front of your right foot, touching your left heel to your right toes.
- Then place your right foot in front of your left foot, touching your right heel to your left toes.
- Continue stepping forward for 20 steps.

Some tips for doing the exercises are to maintain good posture, focus your gaze on a fixed point straight ahead, and bend your knees slightly to avoid hyper-extending them. Conduct the exercises adjacent to a counter or sturdy chair so you can catch your balance if you start to tip.

Online sources also advised me to contact my health-care provider if I had any ailments that might be contributing to fall risk: dizziness, blackouts, memory loss, or vision or hearing problems. Medications that can contribute to balance difficulties include some antidepressants, sedatives, and sleep aids.

I also learned my body is not the only factor contributing to fall risk. My house conditions might be doing it as well. Advice for a creating a safer home environment includes the following:
- Clean up clutter and remove other tripping hazards, such as loose carpet or slippery throw

rugs.
- Make sure your home is well lit, especially your stairways.
- Use non-slip mats in showers and bathtubs. (We learned this one from experience, and installed mats after my husband slipped and fell in our shower.)
- Use a sturdy step stool, not a chair, to reach high places. Even better, store frequently used items lower so you don't need a step stool at all.

If your balance and mobility are limited, it's important to use devices such as a cane or walker. The following devices for your home might be helpful as well: handrails on both sides of stairways, a raised toilet seat or one with armrests, grab bars for the shower or tub—or even a sturdy plastic seat so that you can shower while seated. In this case a handheld shower nozzle is also important.

Some of these items might require a financial investment, but the money will be well spent. Consider it an investment in your independence.

I still can't match Garrison Keillor's feat of standing on one foot for ten seconds with my eyes closed. But I did find a balance standard that was comforting. In your 50s you should be able to stand on one foot (with your eyes open) for 40 seconds. In your 60s, you should be able to do it for 20 seconds, and in your 70s for 10 seconds.

That standard I can meet—and even exceed.

Someday, if I exercise faithfully, maybe, just maybe, I will be able balance on one foot for 10 seconds with my eyes closed.

34 To Laugh or Not to Laugh

While all comedy has an overt meaning, much of it also delivers a hidden, negative message, one we may not consciously recognize or realize we are sending. —Anne McGee-Cooper, et al.

My husband Marlo looked at his smartphone and chuckled.

He turned his phone to show me a photo.

It had a single stalk of corn and the caption, "Corn maze for old people."

I smiled.

Then I teased him. "Marlo, that's ageist!"

He rolled his eyes and headed for his garage workshop.

Alone in the house, I wondered about that joke. Was it indeed ageist?

I tested it by filling in the "old people" slot with other minorities. "Corn maze for blacks." "Corn maze for mentally disabled."

Those jokes were definitely in bad taste. I would not have laughed.

But I had laughed at "Corn maze for old people."

I followed Marlo out to the garage. "I was teasing about the joke being ageist," I said, "but now I'm thinking it might truly be ageist. I would never call that photo a corn maze for people of color."

"I've just been wondering about that, too," he said. "Remember my mother in her 90s? First, she got lost driving to other towns. Then she got lost driving to her hairdresser just a few blocks from home. It wasn't funny."

"It was sad," I said. "Besides, the joke depends on the stereotype that all older people have significant memory issues and get lost easily."

Our conversation ended. Marlo turned to his woodworking project, and I headed for my office, still wondering about the joke.

"It definitely has an ageist component," I thought. "But at the same time there is something hilarious and absurd about the image of a single stalk of corn serving as a corn maze."

I was stuck between the devil and the deep blue sea. If I said the joke wasn't funny, I felt like a grinch. If I laughed at it, I felt guilty for being ageist.

"What makes a joke funny anyway?" I wondered. I googled it and learned that there are multiple theories of humor. Plato and others said we laugh when we feel superior. Freud said we laugh, especially at forbidden subjects, to release pent-up energy. Others said we laugh when there is an incongruity: two things that do not belong together are put together in a surprising way. Still others said we laugh when there is a benign violation of a norm.

So, when I laughed at the single corn stalk being called a corn maze for old people, was I feeling superior to people who couldn't find their way out of a maze? Was I releasing the nervous energy of my own fear of memory loss? Was I laughing at the incongruity of a single stalk of corn serving as a corn maze? I didn't know.

But I was convinced that the joke was ageist. I thought again about the ageism of the stereotype the joke relied on. "Can't I laugh at any jokes about old age?" I wondered. "Do all jokes involving older adults rely on a negative stereotype to work?"

I decided to scour the internet and see if there were any jokes that could pass the ageism test. I adapted the following examples from the *Reader's Digest* site.

. . .

I recently asked a new acquaintance how old his children were. He replied, "My children with my first wife are 44 and 39. With my second wife my kids are 15 and 13."

I exclaimed, "That's quite an age difference!"

He explained, "The older ones didn't give me any grandkids—so I made my own."

. . .

Two older adults, Fred and Sam, went to the movies. A few minutes after it started, Fred heard Sam rustling around, and searching on the floor under his seat. "What are you doing?" asked Fred.

Sam, a little grumpy by this time, replied, "I had a caramel in my mouth, and it dropped out. I can't find it."

Fred told him, "Forget it! It'll be too dirty anyway."

"I can't forget it," said Sam. "My teeth are in it!"

. . .

To my friend's astonishment, a police car pulled up to her house and her elderly grandfather got out. The patrolman explained that her grandfather had been lost in the city park and had asked for help.

"Why, Grandfather," my friend said, "you've been going there for 40 years. How could you get lost?"

He smiled slyly. "I wasn't exactly lost," he admitted. "I just got tired of walking."

. . .

By my standards, the above jokes have passed the ageism test. Either they don't depend on stereotypes, or they turn stereotypes on their heads.

35 In Praise of Naps

The replenishing thing that comes with a nap—you end up with two mornings in a day.
—Pete Hamill, American Journalist

I can't nap.

I have tried to nap.

I have failed.

My husband Marlo is a skilled napper. After lunch most afternoons, he heads for his recliner, tilts it back, and immediately falls asleep for half an hour or so. He wakes up refreshed and ready to face the afternoon with renewed vigor.

Then, at night, he needs less sleep than I do. He usually wakes up after seven hours in bed. I can sleep for ten hours.

I'm embarrassed that I go to bed earlier than he does and get up later.

By napping regularly, Marlo follows the tradition of many famous nappers. Not all of them limited themselves to 30 minutes. Presidents Eisenhower, Kennedy, and Johnson all took two-hour naps in the early afternoon. Winston Churchill's two-hour afternoon naps were so important to him, he brought a bed to the parliament building so he could nap there. Margaret Thatcher also napped daily.

Thomas Edison claimed he only needed three to four hours of sleep per night. He tried to hide his several-hour daytime naps.

Leonardo da Vinci had an unusual sleep schedule, napping for fifteen minutes every four hours.

I have tried to join the ritual of Marlo and these famous people, reading the instructions of napping experts:

- Find a peaceful, dark, and quiet place.
- Select a napping time of early afternoon.
- Nap for just 10-30 minutes so that you don't enter your deep sleep cycle and wake up groggy. Napping for too long can also interfere with nighttime sleep. (Apparently, this posed no a problem for the famous two-hour nappers.)

When Marlo has headed for his recliner, I have tried pulling the blinds in our great room and napping on the couch. I prop a pillow under my head, instruct my body and brain to relax—and lie there wide awake, my brain stubbornly clinging to the "on" setting. There is no risk of my entering the deep sleep cycle. After half an hour I am still wide awake.

The list of napping's benefits increases my desire to nap. Its benefits include:

- Relaxation.
- Reduced fatigue.
- Increased alertness.
- Improved mood.
- Better memory.
- Increased creativity.

The benefits of napping are recognized around the globe. In Japan, sleep cafes provide a place near work for employees to take an afternoon break. In Italy, businesses close for two to three hours in the afternoon for the traditional *pisolino*. Nike, Proctor and Gamble, and Facebook have created rooms for employees to nap.

Did I say I can't nap? That's not totally true.

I can't nap at a planned time. But I can fall asleep at inopportune times.

I can drift off to sleep while reading or working at my computer. While drafting this chapter, I dozed off three times.

I can do the same while watching television. It doesn't matter if the show interests me. I can still drift off without trying.

I can drift back to sleep after my alarm rings. Sometimes I hit the snooze button two or three times—and drift back off to sleep within two seconds of pushing the button. Sometimes I shut the alarm off, telling myself that I will get up in a second, and that second turns into half an hour of extra sleep.

I can sleep in the car—the hum of the car and the vibration from the wheels are soporific for me. Without caffeine, I could drift off to sleep while driving.

But I cannot lie down and take a nap. Yesterday, after falling asleep reading internet printouts, I decided to trick myself into a nap. I took the printouts to the couch to read them there. "I'll pretend I want to stay awake and read," I told myself. "That will trigger the sleep cycle."

It didn't. I read through every page without achieving any shut-eye.

Albert Einstein and Salvador Dali were fans of micro-naps. Both went to sleep seated, holding a key or a spoon in one hand. When they drifted off to sleep, the object clattered to the floor and woke them. Waking during this stage of sleep tapped into the part of their brains with vivid images and sensation. The two men found some of their most creative times occurred this half-awake state. Edison reported the same experience.

I wish my short snoozes were like their micro-naps. Unfortunately, my dozing off doesn't stimulate creativity. It only leaves me sleepy.

Last week, I told a friend about my affliction. She suggested taking my reading to a recliner. Perhaps it would feel more like the chair in which I so easily drift off. It didn't work.

Each day, I continue to experience nap-envy. I stare at my husband in wonder every afternoon as he drifts blissfully off and then wakes energized and alert to face the rest of his day.

36 Play to Win?

We didn't lose the game; we just ran out of time.
  —Vince Lombardi, Football Coach

My competitive father claimed, "There is no reason to play a game if you don't play to win." When he invited family members to play cards with him, he asked, "Want to get beat in a game of gin?"

If we accepted his challenge, we tried our best to find a smart-aleck reply such as, "Well, you can TRY to beat me, but you won't succeed" or "You'll need lots of luck for that."

If he lost several games, he challenged his opponent to a final game, saying, "This one is for ALL the marbles, for the WHOLE enchilada, for the championship of the world."

Over the years, my siblings and I absorbed his standard. We played to win.

When we were kids, this standard sometimes provoked loud arguments during Monopoly games. One brother refused to trade or sell properties unless he gained a significant advantage.

When the game of Risk entered our home, the disagreements became more than parental ears could tolerate. We were soon forbidden to play it.

All the while, Dad maintained his claim. A game was

worth playing only if you played to win.

I accepted Dad's standard. Throughout my life, I played to win. It made games exciting. It added suspense. Would I be able to win this one, or would I be defeated?

Just once, I played to lose. I was a single twenty-something, playing chess with a bachelor in whom I was romantically interested. I was ahead in the game, and didn't want to be. So, I deliberately put my queen in jeopardy. He looked at me, puzzled. In that moment, I knew he had read my ploy. He hesitated, and then captured my queen. He never asked me out again.

I have never deliberately lost a game since then, not even when playing my grandchildren. I simply don't have it in me.

My sister Kathy and her husband John visited us recently. We played lots of Euchre, a card game of bidding and strategy. We played to win. There was high drama on both sides with lots of suspense—glee over bids made, sadness over bids missed. There was rehash over how bids could have been won if cards had been played in different sequences. We kept track of total wins and losses, with the losers wanting to play another game or two for a chance to even the score.

Kathy and John left on a Sunday morning. That evening we invited a neighborhood couple over to play Crokinole—a game similar to Carom—in which accurate shooting of discs wins the game. Crokinole requires accuracy, but not the same level of focus and concentration as Euchre. Our goal was to have a pleasant time and get better acquainted. We took pleasure in each other's good shots, lamented with each other on our misses. After a couple of games, we switched partners and played some more. A few times, my competitive nature appeared, but it felt out of place in this context.

The contrast of the two experiences left me curious

about competitiveness and aging. I googled them with several different search phrases, but found no data on whether competitiveness subsides with age. I did, however, find lists of the benefits of game playing for older adults. These benefits included:
- Stress relief. Doing something pleasurable, like games, releases endorphins which raise our mood and relieve stress. Release of these endorphins also improves our immune systems and helps lower our blood pressure.
- Improved brain function. Whether the game is primarily physical or cognitive, it has a positive impact on our reaction speed and critical thinking skills. It reduces the risk of cognitive decline.
- Improved relationships. It reduces social isolation, loneliness, and depression. It creates bonds with others, including with the younger generations.

Reflecting on the differences between the two gaming experiences, I realized that playing to win interfered with some of the benefits of games. When I finished playing Euchre, I was tense and tired. It had not provided stress relief or improved relationships.

When I finished playing Crokinole, I was energized and had built bonds with our neighbors.

In these later years of my life, fierce competition is becoming less attractive, and collaborative experiences more so.

My father may have been partly right, but I am learning that he was also partly wrong.

37 The Organized Mind

Our brains are inherently good at creating categories.
—Daniel Levitin

This week, I started reading *The Organized Mind* by Daniel Levitin. It was a clear-out-clutter book on steroids! Levitin wrote that an organized environment frees up your mind for creativity and productivity. Given bait like that, I was hooked.

I put down the book after reading Chapter 4, Home Organization, and I was pumped. I could do this! I would never have to hunt for anything again.

Chapter 4 offered a myriad of new organizational motivations and possibilities. The task of organization, according to Levitin, is to provide me with maximum information with the least effort on the part of my brain. We not only need a place for everything and everything in its place; that place needs to be an appropriate one. Store similar things together, or group items that have a similar use. And make the storage location near an object's place of use. Getting organized means gaining control. Don't keep anything you do not use. Most important, however: Have only one place for everything, and ALWAYS use that place. Designating multiple locations for the same item will result in wasting time hunting for it and more difficulty remembering the location.

I immediately decided to resume always using my fanny pack for my cell phone when I was at home, and a special purse compartment for the phone when away from home. I designated my bedside stand for my Kindle, since bed was where I most frequently read it.

Consistent use of these locations required commitment. I found myself absentmindedly putting the phone or Kindle down on the table, the desk, or the entry table without even thinking about it, and then I didn't know where to find them. The solution for that, says Levitin, is mindfulness. Truly being present to a moment rather than functioning on automatic pilot.

I then started organizing my home storage with a file drawer that was crushed full. I removed all folders dated 2021, a removal long overdue. I disposed of most of their contents. Hurrah! My file drawer now boasted some usable space.

My priority the next day was the bathroom cabinet. I was tired of hunting for the nail clipper, face wipes, and Tylenol in the mishmash on the shelves. I got out some plastic storage boxes and started sorting. Each category received its own box: lotions, over-the-counter medications, hairstyling equipment, manicure supplies, etc. Usable items I no longer wanted went into a cardboard box for the local thrift store. I put some scented lotions and soaps (which make me sneeze) into a bag to gift to my daughter-in-law.

Outdated medications I put in a plastic bag for disposal, called a local pharmacy about medication disposal, and learned I could take it to a Pella Police Station drop box.

Organizing that cabinet gobbled an entire afternoon. When I had finished, I paused for what my husband and I have come to call an "admiration stance." It was satisfying to have a place for everything and everything in its place.

Putting things back into the correct bathroom space was easy compared to putting my cell phone and Kindle in place. I used an item, took one step to the cabinet, and put it in place. It's what I always have done, except now that place was more specific.

Having one organized space, I considered new goals. It felt so good to have the bathroom organized; imagine how good it would feel if I organized the whole house!

My closet bulged with clothes. I had not pruned my electronic files in several years. Tangles of electronic supplies lurked in the plastic drawers in the office closet. A mess of cleaning supplies hid under the kitchen sink. Cards and envelopes were crammed in a dresser drawer. The laundry room sported a catchall junk drawer. And I didn't want to begin thinking about my portion of the garage shelving.

Then, as suddenly as it had appeared, my energy burst ended. One organized drawer and one cabinet were all my energy could sustain for the moment. I wanted to write and read. I wanted to play pickleball and do some quilling (crafting with paper coils).

When I am ready for another burst of organizing energy, I will reach for my copy of *The Organized Mind* again.

38 After the Fall

"The most important thing in life is learning how to fall."
— *Jeannette Walls, Author*

It began as an ordinary Friday stop at the grocery store. I walked briskly toward the door, caught my toe on a high section of sidewalk, and was suddenly airborne.

"Get your feet under your body," I told myself. But I was too far gone. I reached my arms earthward to break my fall. They were too weak to hold. My elbows collapsed and the corner of my forehead crashed into the cement. My glasses flew from my face.

Lying on my stomach I took inventory. Pain? My legs felt OK. So did my arms. My forehead throbbed. I sat up and reached for my glasses. Their left temple angled oddly, totally askew. I eased it back almost to its normal angle.

Warm liquid oozed down my face and onto my neck. I touched my cheek. My fingers turned red.

I glanced around. No one in the parking lot. No one in sight anywhere. Good!

I hustled to my car, grabbed some Kleenex, and stanched the flow. As I put pressure on it for a minute or two, the bleeding stopped. The cut must not be deep enough to need stitches. I dried my cheek and neck as best I could.

I decided to skip the grocery store and head for my volunteer work as receptionist at The Well Resource Center. In the bathroom there, I cleaned up and took inventory: a red spot and bruise above my eyebrow, a few bloodstains on my bright-print shirt and black coat, and some minor scrapes on my hands.

To partially conceal the damage, I pulled my bangs down

"I hope no one notices," I thought. I wanted to keep this humiliation private.

No one commented. Not the clients, not my colleagues.

My shift done, I drove home. Would my husband Marlo notice?

He didn't.

I soaked my shirt in cold water and wiped the stains from the black coat. Then I confessed. He empathized. "You were lucky," he said. "It could have been much worse."

I nodded.

We ate out at George's Pizza. Neither the staff nor the acquaintances we passed commented. I was surprised. The bruise above my eye was now swollen and blue.

I went grocery shopping on Saturday. No one commented.

I attended worship on Sunday. No one commented.

It was becoming frustrating. I had a crust above my eye and a bruise surrounding it, and no one said a thing.

I attended Bible studies on Tuesday and Wednesday mornings. By now I was developing a blue-green shiner alongside of my eye. But no one said a thing. "Am I invisible?" I wondered.

I started having bad dreams in which I tumbled down a cliff into an abyss.

Wednesday afternoon I got a haircut and perm. My

bangs now no longer covered the brown scab.

Marlo said, "At tonight's small-group meeting, someone will mention it for sure." BUT STILL NO ONE COMMENTED.

When I had fallen at the grocery store, I had hoped no one would notice. I had looked around after I fell, relieved there was no witness in sight. I was embarrassed. I didn't want to be seen as a frail, elderly person whose sense of balance was failing.

Then, when no one commented for days, I felt cheated of being able to tell the story. Why did I have such mixed feelings about a simple fall?

I did some reading about the aftermath of trauma, an emotional reaction that stems from a potentially harmful event. A fall might, I supposed, evoke a minor traumatic reaction. I discovered a therapy for trauma. Yup, telling the story.

Telling the story, I learned, could be therapeutic. It could:

- Reduce feelings of shame.
- Correct unhelpful beliefs about the event.
- Remove some of an event's emotional power.

Within ten days of my fall, I did get to tell my mishap story to two people besides my husband: my hairdresser and my massage therapist, both of whom, by the nature of their work, got an up close and personal view of the bruising. Both empathized, and both agreed that I had been blessed not to break any bones.

- I became less ashamed.
- I stopped thinking of myself as frail.
- The incident gradually lost its power over me.

I still had the bad dreams of falling, however.

And now, I am telling the story a fourth time—in writing.

Perhaps, after this fourth telling, I will no longer dream I am tumbling into an abyss.

39 High Tech, Low Control

Technology makes it possible for people to gain control over everything, except over technology.
—John Tudor, Baseball Player

It's time for our annual trip to Phoenix to escape the Iowa winter. We have successfully navigated the Vacation-Rentals-by-Owner (VRBO) website and reserved a house in the area and at a price range we wanted.

Our GPS directs us to Sixth Place, but there is no house number that matches the one in our email. We call our housemates, Lee and Marlene, who say they navigated the same issue the previous day and discovered our rental two blocks away. It was on Sixth Street, not Sixth Place, as listed in the information we received.

We arrive, successfully punch the numbers on the screen of the keyless entry lock, and carry in our suitcases.

It's almost time for Des Moines Christian School's substate basketball game, so hooking up our computer to Wi-Fi is a top priority. We search the house for a manual like the ones that have contained this information for our Phoenix rentals for the past ten years. We open every kitchen drawer and cupboard.

No manual. We check the living room, den, bedrooms. No manual. We check the kitchen again. Still no success. We call our host. It's all on the app, he says.

We download the VRBO app and search for Wi-Fi information. The app says to contact your host for the Wi-Fi password. We contact our host again. This time he tells us the password is on the bottom of the modem.

Our companions enter the password and then the URL given them by their son-in-law who is a Des Moines Christian High coach. We settle in to watch the game.

It's a bit chilly in the house. The old thermostat has tape over it. Next to it is a new circular, electronic thermostat, set at 52 degrees. My husband Marlo taps every option on the screen, but cannot find a way to raise the temperature. He googles the thermostat model and discovers that you can raise the temperature by rubbing the circumference of the thermostat in a counterclockwise direction and then tapping it. We set the thermostat on 68 degrees.

During the night our bedroom gets chilly, and we add an extra blanket. The next morning, we discover that the thermostat has reverted to 52 degrees. It reverts to 52 degrees every hour throughout the day. Eventually, Marlo figures out how to set a temperature that will hold for twelve hours instead of just one. He fails to figure out how to reset the temperature permanently.

We master the use of the computerized coffeepot, the washer, and the dryer without incident.

The next morning, we discover a low-tech problem. Birds from the tree near the driveway have pooped all over our Honda Odyssey. This problem is familiar territory: with an old-fashioned rag and a bucket of water Marlo attacks the bird doo-doo.

Meanwhile housemate Marlene begins to suspect that the VRBO app we downloaded might not be the right app. Maybe the owner sent a different app for us to use. She emails him to inquire.

"We are needing instructions about garbage pickup, running the thermostat, departure guidelines, etc. Is there another app we should be using?"

We get the answer: "Once you have booked, you will receive detailed instructions."

Marlene replies: "We have already been here for two days."

We receive three emails in reply:
1. An apology for misunderstanding the first email.
2. An explanation about rubbing the right side of the thermostat counterclockwise to raise the temperature, clockwise to lower the temperature, which we have already figured out. Our host provides no explanation of how to program it rather than reset it every twelve hours.
3. A note that we will receive simple exit instructions the day before our scheduled departure.

There is no information about putting out garbage totes—which has been required of us at previous rentals.

We notice that the neighbors are putting out garbage and recycling totes. We debate putting ours out as well and discover that the gate between the totes and the road is locked. We decide against taking the totes through the house to the street. Later that night we receive a message: a handyman will remove the garbage tomorrow.

At bedtime we rub and tap the thermostat to set it on 68 degrees. When we wake in the morning the house temperature is 66 degrees. We suspect the heat pump is ailing and unable to maintain temperature. We decide to live with an ailing heat pump rather than bother our host again.

We do wish we had someone to guide us through

the electronic jungle.

When we packed our suitcases for this vacation, we should have included a couple of grandchildren.

40 Family Clowns

You don't stop laughing when you grow old; you grow old when you stop laughing. –George Bernard Shaw

When my sons were young, my sister Jan contributed to family reunion fun by putting on bright lipstick, calling herself the Phantom Kisser, and putting a red lip imprint on the cheeks of her nieces and nephews. There were squeals of delight and mock fear as she chased them and kissed their cheeks.

Now she does the same on the rare occasions when she sees my grandchildren. They don't remember all of their great aunts and uncles, but they know the Phantom Kisser, and they wonder if she will pounce the next time they see her.

That's not Jan's only clowning. She has a gorilla costume, complete with a hairy and grinning head. The gorilla has shown up at her grandchildren's homes, peeking in through the windows and ringing the doorbell. The younger children have been scared, but the older ones have consoled them, "Don't worry. That's just Grandma being silly again."

Jan puts a lot of silliness in her life. This past Christmas, she dyed her hair red and wore an elf costume to work, complete with a hat, bright red cheeks, and green shorts with suspenders.

She added tights. "Legs the age of mine do not belong on display," she said.

Last fall when she got a haircut, she put on more makeup than Phyllis Diller, including the false eyelashes, and went to her job claiming to be Janiese, Jan's sister, filling in for the day because Jan had to miss work.

She inherited her clowning from our father, Henry Addink. In his eighties he bought my mother a six-foot teddy bear as a Valentine gift. It sat in a rocking chair in their living room in the years that followed.

Much of the time, Dad's clown moments were unintentional—and a bit dangerous. Once, in midlife, he was alongside the raised hood of his car, trying to start the engine. The car started—in gear. His arm caught on the hood, and he ended up running alongside the car until it was stopped by a house.

He once tried a joke demonstrating his quick draw with a pistol. The joke was supposed to be:

"Want to see my quick draw?" Dad has his hand on the pistol but doesn't move it.

Then, pretending his draw is so fast it was invisible, he says, "Want to see it again?"

Dad executed the first step fine, but when he said, "Want to see it again?" he accidentally pulled the trigger and shot a hole in his shoe.

"Yes, yes!" teased his sons and nephews gathered around him. "Do it again! Do it again!"

They were clowning, but Dad didn't think they were funny.

Neither did he see the humor in the gift they subsequently gave him: a drawing of a target with a toe drawn into the center of the circle. They labeled the poster "Henry Addink Pistol Target."

As for me, I am neither an accidental clown like my father nor a clown-on-purpose like my sister. I am the serious clan member who sets goals and works toward them. I'm good at getting things done, but lack a single ounce of circus performer.

I laugh whenever I read the Jenny Joseph poem about getting old and wearing purple, wearing a red hat that doesn't match, going outside in slippers in the rain, and learning to spit. Of course, I would never do those wacky things. I only laugh at the idea of someone doing them, in the same way I have laughed at my sister and my father.

When Jenny Joseph wrote her poem at age 29, she suggested she might "practice a little now" so people wouldn't be too surprised when suddenly she was old and started to wear purple.

I don't know exactly when it happened, but I am suddenly old. I didn't practice unconventional living when I was young, and suspect I won't start now. I shall not make up for the sobriety of my youth: I shall continue on the path on which I began.

Once, though, at around age 35 or so, I stepped out of my conventional role. My husband was working in our backyard vegetable garden. I checked around for onlookers. There were none, so I pulled down my britches and mooned him through the patio door. He stopped weeding in total shock, guffawed, and came to the house, still laughing.

"I cannot believe you did that!" he said. Neither could our friends and acquaintances when he told them the tale.

I may be the plain-Jane, serious member of the clan, but a single clown gene was hiding in me somewhere. Maybe that was my "little practice" before I turned old.

However, I don't intend to wear purple and learn to spit. A clown moment will likely never surface in me again. I'm not the family clown, but that's ok. I'm the family narrator instead, telling the clown stories to share the laughter and the fun.

41 Losing Multitasking Skills

I'm so good at multitasking that I can listen, ignore, and forget all at once. —Facebook Meme

"Don't talk to me now," my husband Marlo says as we approach an exit on the interstate in heavy traffic. At that point he needs to focus on driving and doesn't want the distraction of a conversation.

Decades ago, he carried on a conversation while making driving decisions, but that ability to do both at the same time has faded. His experience is typical. Studies have shown that, as the years go by, the multitasking ability of older adults fades. We are no longer as good at it as when we were younger.

Well, sort of.

It turns out none of us are as good at it as we might think.

Earl Miller, MIT neuroscientist and expert on divided attention, says our brains are not made to multitask well. "When people think they're multitasking, they're actually just switching from one task to another very rapidly. And every time they do, there's a cognitive cost in doing so."

Already in the 1990s, researchers found when people switched back and forth between two tasks, they were slower than when they completed first one task and then another. The more complex the tasks were, the more time they lost when switching tasks.

In addition, researchers found that task switching resulted in less accurate work. When switching tasks, we make more mistakes.

Retention of information while task switching is also poorer. College students who were on social media while doing homework completed that homework more slowly and got poorer grades. They also retained less information from lectures if they used social media during those lectures.

When multitasking is habitual, it can affect how the brain works, causing it to retain less information. We become less able to focus on one task, even when we want to mono-task.

When older adults have more trouble with multiple tasks, their difficulty actually comes in switching between tasks. We have more difficulty disengaging from an interruption, and then more difficulty re-engaging with the original task. If we answer a phone call when headed for the bedroom, we have more difficulty leaving that call behind and more difficulty retrieving why we were headed to the bedroom in the first place. Just as aging bodies are stiffer and less mobile, so aging brains have more difficulty maneuvering.

We also have more brain chatter than at younger ages. Brain scans of children and young adults show them able to concentrate on just one item with their full attention; older adults have more scattered thoughts in general. On a walk with a friend, we might also be thinking of what's on our grocery list. A nurse said when she worked in war zones decades ago, she could give her full attention to patients, treating the ones in most urgent need of medical care and going from patient to patient in rapid succession. Now she would also be reflecting on the morality of war.

The truth is this: the attempt to multitask was never

good for us, not even when we were young. So, rather than lamenting our inability to switch rapidly from one task to another, we can work on becoming skilled mono-taskers, which is more efficient anyway:

- We can give ourselves permission to work on one task at a time, choose the most important task in this moment, and focus on it.
- We can chunk tasks, dividing them up into categories. Instead of checking emails or texts multiple times per day, we can designate a few times a day for those tasks, and let them accumulate until our next designated time.
- If we really feel we cannot get everything done without doing multiple tasks at once, perhaps we should remove a few commitments from our lives. We can do a little less and do it better.
- We can practice focus. We can take several deep breaths and choose one thing to focus on for the next 20-30 minutes, setting a timer for accountability. Then we can take a five-minute break and repeat the process.

There's a nonintellectual benefit to single-tasking as well. When we slow down and focus on one task at a time, we become mindful; we become present to the moment. And that has a wide range of benefits, including combating depression, anxiety, and chronic pain.

Perhaps the growing need to do one thing at a time is a blessing in disguise.

42 Phone Call

A teacher affects eternity; he can never tell where his influence stops. —Henry Brooks Adams, American Historian

Monday morning, I find a message from The Write Place in my phone mail. "Ed Boer left a message for you. He'd like to talk with you about your book *Child of the Plains*. If you want to talk with him, his number is . . . ."

The Write Place is a business I formerly owned and managed. Ed must have googled me, failed to find my personal phone number, and found my former connection to The Write Place.

Ed Boer? Can he possibly be the Ed Boer who was my junior high English teacher in Orange City, Iowa, more than six decades ago? That would be amazing. I have often wondered about him over the years.

I eagerly punch the phone number into my cell phone, and a clear tenor voice, almost the same as I remember from decades ago, greets me.

"Is this Ed Boer?"

"Yes," he says.

"Is this the same Ed Boer who taught English in northwest Iowa in the 1960s?" I ask. I hold my breath.

He says yes, and I introduce myself. "I've been hoping you would call," he says. "I enjoyed your book and identified with it." Like me, he grew up on a farm near a small northwest Iowa town, and his small-Iowa-town experiences were very similar to mine. The book brought back many memories for him, he says.

His background is new information for me. In junior high I saw him simply as "Mr. Boer" who appeared out of nowhere at the beginning of the school year. I knew he had children, because I babysat for them. I knew he was a softball pitcher because my umpire father told me that. But I never considered him as having a childhood.

His presence in the classroom was memorable. He taught us sentence structures with clarity and precision. He organized our school's first-ever interpretive reading contest. I chose O. Henry's short story "The Whirligig of Life," for which I enjoyed trying to imitate a hillbilly drawl. That story stayed in my papers until I turned 50. In fact, it may still be buried in my memorabilia.

Mr. Boer also introduced us to the classics, walking us through Sophocles' Greek drama *Antigone*. That play was an ambitious undertaking for 25 squirrelly junior high students. (It may have been a simplified version. At the time, though, I believed I was reading Sophocles.)

When I suggest a Sophocles undertaking was daring, Ed replies, "But your class was an unusual one. I didn't realize how unusual that class was until I taught other classes in subsequent years."

I have never thought of my class as unusual, but as Ed and I chat we recall the careers of various members of that group. I realize how academically gifted some of my classmates were, going on to become doctors, architects, teachers, and contractors.

"Based on your book, I concluded you didn't exactly like junior high," he says.

"I liked school academically," I say. "I just didn't fit socially. I didn't become comfortable in my own skin until I reached college."

Then I tell him how his grammar lessons carried me through high school, and how his encouragement to study English led to a college major and a career in words. Ed Boer's influence had been something I wished I could tell him about over the years, but I had never before had a chance.

We talk about the intervening years. He moved to Michigan, where he became half-time school librarian and half-time middle-school English teacher. I taught high school and college English and did various kinds of writing—including founding The Write Place.

We discuss people from our shared past and what we are doing in retirement. We discover we both have become part-time performers. He has become a storyteller—sharing both folk tales and true stories with different clubs and groups in Florida where he retired.

"Do you have the stories memorized?" I ask.

"Almost," he says.

"That would terrify me," I say. "I do readings for groups, but I want the script in front of me when I'm performing."

Not Ed. He wants to rely on the story in his head.

He thanks me for calling. He says it has been a highlight in his day.

It has been a highlight for me as well.

At age 74, to get a chance to tell a former teacher how he helped to shape my life is a rare privilege, indeed.

43 The Great Unretirement

You are never too old to set a new goal or dream a new dream. —C.S. Lewis

During the pandemic, 8 million people lost or left their jobs. The percentage of retirement-age people in the work force dropped. But, thanks to a waning pandemic, a thriving job market, and a soaring cost of living (8.7 percent in 2022), retirees are returning to work in what some call "The Great Unretirement."

The percentage of retirement-age people now in the workforce has almost reached the pre-pandemic levels. Twenty percent of them are currently working. In one survey, 68 percent of those who retired during the pandemic said they were considering returning to work.

Twenty-seven percent of retirees returning to employment say they are doing so for financial reasons. Some feel the pinch of inflation. Others realize that their retirements are underfunded. They have not saved enough to last through an extended retirement period.

Some retirees choose jobs in grocery stores, bookstores, or movie theaters, which offer them discounts on merchandise, and so they save on expenses.

Not everyone returns to work for financial reasons, however. Sixty percent of those returning to employment say they are looking for something to do. Endless recreational time looked good from a distance, but some retirees find themselves bored with too much time on their hands. Some want a way to feel useful. Others like the idea of doing something and getting paid for it.

Although people rarely think of physical health as a reason to return to work or continue working, there is evidence of its physical benefits. A job in which you are physically active can contribute to fitness and weight loss. Working is more beneficial to health than watching TV all day every day. One study reveals people who work one year beyond age 65 have an 11 percent lower risk of death than those who retire at 65.

Employment can provide needed social interaction that can lift your spirits and build a support system. And there is evidence that having an active social life contributes to healthy aging.

A job also reduces cognitive decline, helping us to stay mentally sharp. It provides an opportunity to both mentor and be mentored. A study of nearly half a million people in France revealed that for each additional year of work, the risk of dementia was reduced by 3.2 percent.

People who return to a job are also contributing to the greater good through their work, and it helps boost both the economy and Social Security. Forty-two percent of retirees say having a purpose is crucial to them. Often, they choose to work for nonprofits, in the educational system, or as coaches.

Some retirees turn a lifelong hobby or personal activity into a part-time income. Others leverage their previous job skills in new jobs or become consultants in their area of expertise.

In a robust job market, employers value mature

staff members, who tend to be skilled at problem solving, as well as dependable and loyal. The options of part-time employment and working from home have both expanded. Some people who are unretiring appreciate avoiding the hassle and cost of commuting to jobs. For others the social benefit of in-person work outweighs the cost.

If you retired before reaching your full retirement age, however, returning to employment may reduce your Social Security income. It may also put you in a higher tax bracket. Consult a financial adviser about the financial impact of returning to work if you have not yet reached full retirement age.

Unretiring is not for everyone, but some older adults find it adds to their lives financially, personally, and socially.

44 Accepting Limits

Learn to accept your limits, and you'll be a happier person.
—David D. Burns, Psychiatrist

Once, when my 88-year-old mother forgot a fact (I have forgotten what it was), she threw a shoe across the room in frustration. Dad, age 90, looked at her and said gently, "It is no shame to forget, Mary. When you get old, you forget sometimes. I forget, too."

But his words were no consolation to her. Dad had accepted this aging loss. My mother had not.

We are all getting older. We are aging. Advisers on aging with grace say a key is acceptance.

There are different forms of acceptance. When we accept a gift, we willingly receive it. When we accept pain, we endure it without further protest. When we accept a fact, we recognize it as true. And when we accept a responsibility, we agree to undertake it.

In accepting aging, I think all four of these variations are present. We willingly receive it, we endure it without protest, we recognize it is true, and we agree to undergo the process.

We have no choice about whether or not we will age. Aging is inevitable.

To deny the reality of aging is the height of foolishness. No series of facelifts and tummy tucks and toupees can stop the calendar. We can delay the appearance of aging, but time marches on.

We can delay some of the effects of aging through exercise and healthy eating and staying active mentally and socially. But we cannot stop the biological clock. It keeps on ticking.

Our choice is whether we will accept aging or spend our time fighting it, being angry about it, and eventually growing depressed, anxious, or bitter.

Acceptance of aging, like acceptance of any difficulty in life, is not easy, is not instant, and is not once-and-done.

When one accepts, one may still have pain, but not the unnecessary pain of resentment and self-pity.

Psychologist Marsha Linehan says radical acceptance is a way of tolerating distress. Her definition of radical acceptance: "It's when you stop fighting reality, stop throwing tantrums because reality is not the way you want it, and let go of bitterness."

That's what I'd like to do. That's what I need to do. Over and over again.

There is a necessary balance, though, between acceptance and resistance. You can accept aging and still resist its effects by exercising, eating well, and staying socially active. The balance is like the serenity prayer: God grant me the grace to accept the things I cannot change, the power to change the things I can, and the wisdom to know the difference.

Having realistic expectations is another term for this balance.

One person who wrote about accepting aging spent almost all of her words on staying active and staying healthy. She almost denied the need for acceptance.

In realism, not denial, lies the path to acceptance. We shouldn't expect the worst—it could become a self-fulfilling prophecy. But at the same time, we recognize our minds and bodies have more limitations than they did at age 20. A key is to accept limitations calmly, without clicking into a fight-or-flight response. In balance lies the ability to embrace our past without trying to relive it, to accept our future without being terrified of it. We can be proud of our past achievements and grateful for our current survival. We can fight the negative attitude toward aging, remembering that we are loved.

At 90 my father learned that lung cancer limited his life expectancy to four months. He wept. We did too.

In the days that followed Dad's diagnosis, he found a path to acceptance by living each day as it came. He was an internal processor. He didn't wear his heart on his sleeve, but I saw him come out of his depression and take an interest in his now-more-limited life. We wheeled him to the car and took him on outings—to see the demolition of the local grain elevator, to see the progress on the new Casey's store, to experience the pleasure of a soft-serve ice cream cone. He cherished each experience, absorbing it with eagerness. He was awed by the power of the wrecking ball and amazed by the speed of the construction. He relished the ice cream cone. His gratitude for small daily gifts enhanced his acceptance.

He is a role model for me, and perhaps for us all.

45 On Pride and Technology

Once a new technology rolls over you, if you're not part of the steamroller, you're part of the road. —Stewart Brand, Writer

SUNDAY 10 a.m. As our pastor introduces his message, he asks each of us to recall a repeated sin. "Pride," I think. "Yes, pride." On the way home from church, I tell my husband Marlo which repeated sin came to mind.

WEDNESDAY 1 p.m. My husband and I decide to save money by switching cell phone carriers. The Consumer Cellular sales person tells us he will send us new SIM cards. We will need to open the SIM card tray and make a switch. It's a simple process, he says. The tray is a rectangular cutaway on the narrow edge of the phone. It can be opened by inserting a needle or paper clip into the small hole adjacent to it.

After the phone call I examine all the narrow edges of my Moto G7. I find neither a SIM tray rectangle nor a small hole. I put it under brighter light. No tray. I try a magnifying glass. No tray.

"Do you have a plastic case around it?" asks my husband Marlo. He has one surrounding his phone.

"No," I say, "I just have a leather case glued to the backside. It opens and does not cover the narrow edges."

We google "open SIM tray on Moto G7" and watch a YouTube video that shows the location of the SIM tray and demonstrates how to open it.

I see no SIM tray in that location.

We watch several more YouTube videos. Same story.

WEDNESDAY 2 p.m. I call Motorola tech support. The customer service rep tells me the tray is either on the left side or the top right side. I tell her there is no SIM tray visible in either location. She tells me it has to be there. She asks if I have a plastic cover. I tell her no. She says maybe I have poor eyesight and can't see the tray and hole. The conversation becomes heated. She tells me she can't help me via phone. I will need to take it to some sort of Best Buy store and get in-person help.

The nearest Best Buy is an hour away in Des Moines.

WEDNESDAY 3 p.m. I call Consumer Cellular tech support. We walk through the same scenario. No, my phone doesn't have a plastic case. No, there is no tray visible on any narrow edge of the phone. After several rounds, she tells me I need to go to a Target Consumer Cellular outlet near me, but make sure a phone technician will be available upon my arrival.

The nearest Target with a technician available tomorrow is an hour away in Ankeny.

WEDNESDAY 4 p.m. I call my brother, who recently retired from his ownership of several uBreakiFix phone repair shops in the Midwest. We walk through the same scenario. No, I have no plastic case; no, there are no SIM tray and hole visible. He has more patience with me than tech support. I clean all edges of the phone with a damp cloth. No SIM tray appears. I email him photos of all edges of the phone. No SIM tray is visible to him either. He runs out of time—he needs to take his granddaughter to an event.

WEDNESDAY 5 p.m. I wash the edges again. I study the phone again under a bright light with a magnifying glass. I try the magnifying feature of my husband's cell phone camera. No SIM tray appears.

THURSDAY 2 p.m. I hand my phone to the technician at the Ankeny Target store and explain my problem. She holds the phone, puts her manicured fingers on the narrow edge of the phone, and asks, "Do you mind?"

"Do I mind what?" I ask.

"Do you mind if I remove the plastic cover?"

"It has a plastic cover?!" I exclaim. I mutter to go ahead.

She deftly removes a thin plastic cover that encases all narrow edges of the phone. It is glued to the leather cover which I had forgotten had a plastic component.

She shows me the SIM tray, demonstrates how to open it, and replaces the plastic cover.

I thank her and slink out of the store.

THURSDAY 3 p.m. My husband asks me, "Was that a lesson in humility?" I look at him, puzzled, and he clarifies. "Does that help you a little with that pride problem you mentioned last Sunday?"

I clutch my cell phone in its plastic case. Head held high, I don't deign to answer.

46 The Benefits of Writing Your Story

The worst part of holding the memories is not the pain. It's the loneliness of it. Memories need to be shared. —Lois Lowry

As a writer, I often hear remarks like this: "My children/grandchildren want me to write my memories for them." If the speaker is someone younger than I am, they often say, "I wish my parents/grandparents would write about their lives for us."

Almost as often, I hear statements of regret, "My kids want me to write about my life, but I can't seem to get started on it." After parents/grandparents have died, their descendants say, "If only we had a record of their lives. There's so much we don't know."

My husband's great-grandfather left a record for future generations without really intending to. An immigrant to the United States in the 1800s, he wrote a record of his experiences, not for future generations, but for his peers in the Netherlands who were considering emigrating. He wrote it, of course, in Dutch. But a grandchild recognized its value for descendants, had it translated into English, and ran off mimeographed copies for his family. I later edited the document and published it as the book *My America* by E.J.G. Bloemendaal. Scores of his descendants have since ordered it from Amazon and enjoyed learning about his life as a farmer in the Midwest in the 19th century.

E.J.G. accomplished what many of us fail to do because he had a reason to write. We don't have the same reason to write as he did, but we have many other good reasons to write the memories of our lives.

One is to leave a record of our lives as a legacy for those who come later. Perhaps there are stories we don't want to be lost. Perhaps there are values and advice we would like to pass on. I just finished editing a manuscript for a woman who wanted to share her Christian faith with future generations. She shared stories of both the hard and the happy moments in her life, and concluded her writing with this advice which she had mentioned several times in her writing: "Stand up! Stand strong! But kneel first."

Writing our memories is not something to do solely for future generations, however. It is also something we can do for ourselves. Perhaps when we realize this double reason for writing about our lives, it will kindle in us the fire to write the stories within us.

For many, writing about our lives provides the pleasure of remembering. That pleasure is good for us. Studies have shown reminiscing can ease depression and lower blood pressure. But even without the health benefit, it is just plain fun. Especially pleasant, I think, is writing the memories of our early years and young adulthood. Those are the memories that are clearest to us and the memories which interest our children and grandchildren the most.

Once we start jotting down memories of times gone by, we find one memory leads to another, and we gradually remember more and more details. What our dog's fur felt like, the sound of his high-pitched bark. How the doctor's office smelled as we waited an hour for an appointment to have our tonsils checked. So, writing down our memories can increase our memory bank and increase our pleasure as well.

In writing the story of our lives we also clarify our understanding of it. In the opening of his memoir *Looking Back*, my husband Marlo wrote he could be golfing, practicing music, woodworking, or playing gin, but instead he was writing. Why? "It will help me recall my experiences and perhaps give me new perspectives on my life." He went on to say he was also writing to leave a record.

Part of that new perspective on the past can be the healing of old wounds. The first version of my memoir *Child of the Plains* included my venting about childhood pain. It included pages of self-pity and anger that would be of no use to future generations. However, they were of use to me. Writing helped me heal some childhood wounds. That version of the memoir languished on my computer for four years. Then I was ready to write a version which had readers in mind instead of being simply for my own therapy.

Some people don't try to write their stories because they think they are not good enough writers. But memories written for future generations do not have to be great literature. Future readers will value it, whatever its literary level. Knowing it will be valued might help you get started writing.

Even though we know the many good reasons for writing our life stories, we still may be stopped by simply not knowing how to do it. That "how" will be the topic of the next chapter.

47 How to Start Writing Your Memories

I write because I don't know what I think until I read what I say. —Flannery O'Connor

Last week I wrote about why we should write our memories. This week we will look at how to do that. I think the reason many of us don't write about our lives is that the project seems overwhelming. Writing 100 to 200 pages is an insurmountable rocky mountain that we need to climb barefoot. When we face a blank page, terror strikes.

That fear is common—even among professional writers. When I sit down to start writing, suddenly I feel thirsty. I get a drink of water. Then I realize I need to check my email. I clean my email inbox. Then Facebook calls. . . . I keep procrastinating until I pretend to tie myself to my chair, open the computer to my writing program, and type that first sentence. Other writers may write that first sentence with a pen or pencil. And once that first sentence or two is on paper, writing is more doable than our fears have made us believe.

One process that helps to overcome the fear of the blank page is freewriting. To freewrite we set a timer for 10 minutes and simply type or write whatever pops into our mind next. We can even dictate it using text-to-speech software. If that first thought is, "I can't think of anything to write," we simply write that sentence. If our back itches, we write about that. The only rule for freewriting is that we keep the words flowing. It doesn't have to be profound or organized. It doesn't even need to make sense. We are just practicing putting words on paper. The freewriting exercise has helped many of my writing students overcome their fear of a blank page.

While freewriting, we need to give ourselves permission to make errors. At this stage we don't worry about spelling, grammar, or punctuation. The goal is simply to put a stream of words on paper. I like to imagine I am locking my editor self into a closet and not letting her out until a later stage in the writing process. I tell her that her turn will come, but that turn is not now, and then I turn the key in the lock. I don't listen to her no matter how much she whines or shouts.

If you are a perfectionist when you write, deliberately make two errors in the first couple of sentences. Then you've already made some errors, so more won't matter! You've already demonstrated you can move forward despite imperfection.

Another way to overcome the fear of the huge mountain of writing about your entire life is to create an outline of some incidents in each decade of your life and then choose one of them to write about. Write about a small piece of the puzzle. And when you've created enough puzzle pieces you can figure out how to put them together.

If creating an outline is too intimidating, you might want to try writing the answers in guide books that ask you specific questions about your life and provide space for you to answer. In your computer's search engine, type "life story journal with prompts" and many options will pop up. These books have the advantage of breaking your story into manageable bits, but sometimes they don't allow enough space for a longer story.

If you want more freedom, but need questions to get you started, search the term "memoir writing prompts" and lots of pages with questions to spark writing will be available to you. You can choose the questions that spark a memory and start there.

Another way to get started is to find and gather information. In writing a memoir, we need not rely totally on our memories. We can go through old diaries, old pictures, old news clippings, and family scrap books. We can also question our siblings—and any previous-generation relatives who are still living.

When I was working on my memoir, I interviewed a ninety-year-old uncle, and he remembered lots of details about the farm on which he and my mother grew up and their activities as children. He also had several memories of my grandmother which provided insight into her life as the mother of eleven children. He had memories of my great-grandfather, who lived with my grandparents after he was widowed.

Many of us live with myths about writing that make writing more difficult. Below are some common myths and the truth about each of them:

- Myth: You have to write Chapter 1 first.
  Fact: You can start anywhere and reorder the pieces later.
- Myth: You have to write it right the first time.
  Fact: Almost everything you read was rewritten and edited several times.
- Myth: You have to write every detail of your life.
  Fact: You can choose to focus on just part of your life, such as your childhood. Or you can cover the important and memorable parts of your entire life.
- Myth: You have to be a really good writer to do this.
  Fact: Your story will be treasured because you

wrote it, not because of your writing qualifications.
- Myth: You have to be inspired when you write. Fact: You have to be disciplined to write. You glue yourself to the chair and start putting down words whether you are inspired at the moment or not.

So, if you eventually get 100 to 200 pages on paper and you are ready for the next step, what do you do? I will answer that question in the next chapter.

48 How to Polish and Publish Your Writing

It is perfectly okay to write garbage, as long as you edit brilliantly. —C. J. Cherryh, American Writer

In the last chapter, when we looked at how to start writing your memories, length limits did not allow for one final tip: form a writing group. There are different kinds of writing groups. The group I belong to has four to six members. We meet every two weeks. Then, on the alternate week we email our submissions to the other members of the group. Group accountability is a great way to motivate writing and to improve it.

Useful feedback to give each other is "movies of your mind." Tell the writer what happens inside of you at different points in the writing:

- "I was sad here."
- "I was confused here."
- "I could/couldn't picture this scene."
- "I wanted to know more here."
- etc.

The readers do not tell the writer how to fix the writing; they simply tell the writer what their responses are, and the writer then makes decisions about how to improve the writing.

In editing your work, it is good to move from the big

picture to the details. Questions to ask yourself are: Is this in the order I want it? Does it have an interesting beginning? Are there places I need to add more information? Are there places where it gets bogged down in the details? Did I use vivid and specific words? Are there words that are not needed? Does it have a sense of ending or just trail off?

The last part of editing (and the one people often make the mistake of starting with) is to check the spelling, grammar, and punctuation. If you understand grammar and punctuation, read your work aloud slowly to check for errors. You can also use the spelling and grammar check functions of your word processing program, or find an online program to help you with this. If your spelling, grammar, and punctuation skills are weak, ask someone with these skills to proofread it for you.

Note: the above description of editing is short, but editing is time consuming. Editing often takes me more than twice the amount of time required to create a first draft.

Once you have polished your writing, you are ready to publish—but that doesn't necessarily mean publishing it as an actual book.

Even if you never polish your rough drafts, your notebooks of those drafts will still have value for your descendants. After my mother died, we found some of her notebooks in which she had handwritten her thoughts and memories, and we appreciated the insights these records provided for us.

If you have edited and polished your drafts, you can assemble your pages in a three-ring binder. If you want more than one copy, you can photocopy the pages and make as many binders as you wish.

As an alternative, you can have your pages photocopied and spiral-bound by a local printer for a very modest fee. I did this with a book of my poems that I wanted to make available for descendants.

If you have your heart set on a bound book, you have several choices. The least expensive choice is to go online to Kindle Direct Publishing and do the technical work of laying it out in book format, creating a cover, and uploading it—at no cost. You can then purchase copies of the book from Amazon at a reasonable cost. Although this is free, it takes a fair amount of labor and learning. Kindle Direct Publishing provides step-by-step instructions for creating the book and cover, but some technical skills are required to follow the instructions. My husband and I both followed this route when we published our memoirs, *Child of the Plains* and *Looking Back*, both available on Amazon.

You can also take your electronic files to a printer for cover design, layout, and printing and ask for a price quote for creating the number of copies you would like. A student from one of my memoir-writing classes chose this route, and it cost her $1000 for thirty or so paperback copies of her book.

Finally, you can take your electronic files to a company that helps people self-publish their books and ask for a price quote for the range of services you want, such as editing, proofreading, cover design, layout, and printing. (Beware of companies who lure customers by promising them the riches of launching a best seller. Best sellers are almost impossible to achieve.) One Pella-based company that provides these services without promising a best seller is The Write Place. Using this kind of service will cost several thousand dollars, and is dependent on the size of your book and the range of services you request.

And now this series of three chapters about writing, polishing, and publishing your memoir is complete.

49 Coping Devices for Aging Losses

For people without disabilities, technology makes things easier. For people with disabilities, technology makes things possible. —IBM Training Manual

In past chapters we have looked at how to delay physical and cognitive losses, and there are many ways to do that. But in the end, some losses are likely, even though they can be postponed and slowed. When that happens, there are many devices which can help us continue with both the activities of daily living and the activities that bring us pleasure.

If our balance begins to weaken or our legs no longer function well, we can make use of walking aids. For starters we can make use of a cane. Consult with a physical therapist or other health care professional about the choice and use of a cane. Some studies indicate that 70 percent of cane users either have the wrong-length cane or fail to use it correctly. Also available are walking poles. Walking with a pair of these helps greatly with lateral stability. When more support is needed, a walker provides multiple points of support while walking and standing.

It can be difficult to accept the need for walking assistance, but the alternative is falling, which is dangerous. Falling is the leading injury-related cause of death in older adults.

Walking in our homes can also be made safer by lighting them well and removing area rugs and electric cords, which can be tripping hazards. Install nightlights so you can see the path from bed to bathroom.

Specialized handles can attach to your bed to make getting in and out of bed safer. (Guardrails can prevent you from rolling out and onto the floor.) Specialized handles are also available for getting in and out of cars. Another device can sit atop your toilet to raise the seat height. Some of these toilet devices even come with rails to help you push yourself up.

Bathing can be made safer by installing a walk-in shower, putting down a non-slip mat, and adding a safety rail. Some people also find that they are more secure seated in a shower chair and using a handheld showerhead.

If using our hands is difficult because of shakiness or arthritis, a glass with a straw or a cup with a lid and spout can make drinking easier. It is also possible to get mugs with two handles instead of one. Utensils are available with large, easy-to-hold handles, and some are even angled to make it easier to put the food into our mouths.

Buttonhooks and zipper pulls make fastening garments easier. Several sock-aid designs reduce the amount of bending necessary to put on socks. We can remove stubborn lids with a twist-off device. A reacher (a long pole with a grabber at one end) can help us pick up something that has fallen to the floor.

When small print becomes more difficult to read, and regular eyeglasses don't do the trick, a lighted magnifying glass is useful for reading pill bottles, maps, and recipes. Large-print books are available from local libraries, and the size of print can be enlarged for any electronic book. We can also enlarge the print on our computer screens.

Hearing aids are the typical solution to hearing loss,

but in addition it is possible to get telephones with higher-volume speakers. (Phones with over-sized push buttons are also available.) In many cases, hearing aids can receive the audio signal directly from the television and telephone through Bluetooth technology.

For cognitive and memory loss, one of the best tools is low tech and has been around for decades: a pencil. Making lists—shopping lists, to-do lists, names-of-acquaintances lists—can relieve us of the pressure of needing to remember. Setting a timer to ring when we need to leave for an appointment can also be helpful. And checking the calendar each morning to remind us of the schedule for the day can be useful as well. We can then set timers for reminders as needed. Pill dispensers with beepers can remind us to take medications as prescribed.

None of us needs all of these devices. But it is important to know that many devices are available. And they are easy to find online with a simple Google search.

The goal of all these devices is our safety, along with our independence. Both of these have very high value. Knowing about the available devices can help us stay safe and independent longer. That's good news for all of us.

50 For Further Reading

We read books to find out who we are. What other people, real or imaginary, do and think and feel . . . is an essential guide to our understanding of what we ourselves are and may become." – Ursula K. LeGuin, American Author

During the year of writing this book, I have accumulated thirty-some books on aging. Not all of them are equally compelling or useful. Not all of them were published recently. Most of them I bought used from abebooks.com.

Today, I'll tell you about a few of my favorites, in case you want to do further reading.

The most delightful of the books is Garrison Keillor's *Serenity at 70, Gaiety at 80: Why You Should Keep on Getting Older.* It begins, "My life is so good at 79 I wonder why I waited this long to get here, so much of what I know would've been useful in my forties. . . . The world belongs to the young, I am only a tourist, and I love being a foreigner in America." It continues in this light-hearted tone, similar to that of the tales he told about Lake Wobegon in his NPR radio show *A Prairie Home Companion.*

For something a bit feistier, try *This Chair Rocks: A Manifesto against Ageism* by Ashton Applewhite. It is energetic, funny, and packed with information. It traces Applewhite's journey as she became a pro-aging radical. Throughout the book she challenges myth after myth about late life.

Two books that feature the positive side of aging are *Life Gets Better* by Wendy Lustbader and *The Happiness Curve* by Jonathan Rauch. Lustbader recounts the unexpected pleasures of growing older. She says youth can be a time of tension and confusion, and as we grow older, we gain self-knowledge and confidence. Rauch says life gets better after 50. He maintains happiness follows a U-shaped curve, declining from the optimism of youth, slumping in middle age, and rising again in our 50s. He demonstrates how the ordeal of the midlife slump restarts our values, leading to a rebirth of gratitude.

Brain Rules for Aging Well by John Medina provides ten principles for staying vital, happy, and sharp. It is part of his "brain rules" series for the different stages of life. Among the topics he covers are friendships, happiness, stress, memory, mind, food, exercise, and sleep.

In *The Big Shift* Marc Freedman targets readers who are navigating the new stage beyond midlife. His book is designed to help transform a midlife crisis into a midlife opportunity. One of his suggestions is a gap year for grownups, taking a year—as young people sometimes do—for reflection, renewal, and redirection. He recommends forging a new map of life, which is tailored to our longer life spans.

Paul H. Irving's topic is the aging population. *The Upside of Aging* looks at how longer lives are changing the world of health, work, innovation, policy, and purpose. His book is geared for readers in those sectors of society who work with the aging demographic. Each chapter is written by an expert in a different dimension of aging.

For those who are part of the Christian faith tradition, *Third Calling* by Richard and Leona

Bergstrom helps answer the question, "What are you doing the rest of your life?" Their work has been described as "Biblically-based, challenging, and very practical." Throughout the book they make the case that each of us is created and designed for a special purpose, and we have an obligation to fulfill that purpose well.

Two classic volumes, both by medical doctors, are *The Art of Aging* by Sherwin B. Nuland and *The Denial of Aging* by Muriel R. Gillick. Nuland has a scientist's passion for truth and a humanist's understanding of the heart. He writes with candor and insight about the variability of the aging experience. He covers how our body and mind age and how we make choices as we grow older. He includes case studies of people who overcame some of the challenges of aging. Muriel Gillick is also frank about aging, starting with the fact that eating right and exercising may delay the effects of aging, but they will not prevent it. She lays out action plans for individuals and for communities, suggesting we should not only do what we can to maintain our health, but we should also vote and organize for appropriate housing options, for employment that uses the skills of older adults, and for better management of disabilities and chronic disease.

Finally, I recommend *Taking Retirement* by Carl H. Klaus, founder of the nonfiction program at the University of Iowa. In surprisingly absorbing fashion, Klaus keeps a daily diary of his bittersweet adjustment to retirement after a lifetime of teaching. He says he wrote it "so that I could genuinely take retirement rather than feel as if it were taking me unawares."

These are a few of the writers who have enriched and illumined my journey during retirement. I hope some of them do the same for you.

51 Happy Retirees

The longer I live, the more beautiful life becomes.
—Frank Lloyd Wright

Retirement living is usually considered a time of joy and freedom, and it often is. However, it is a major life change and requires adjustment, planning, and making choices. For some retirees, this season of life is a time of sadness. What makes the difference? What contributes to a happy retirement?

Two factors of entry into retirement have an impact. People who retired voluntarily are more likely to be happy in retirement than those forced into it by health issues or employers. And people who retire in stages rather than quitting cold turkey also have an easier time adjusting to the change. According to marriage and family therapist Kevin Coleman, retirement employment is usually part-time and less stressful than a retiree's previous job. He also advises, "Find some work that you take pride in and find intrinsically meaningful." Retirees who had bridge employment in their fields had better mental health than those who immediately retired fully.

When they think of a good retirement, many think

first of a solid financial footing. They consult with a financial adviser before retirement and work through the math. Have they accumulated the finances to continue the lifestyle to which they are accustomed? Some discover they may need to work a few more years than they expected, or work part-time in retirement. Others learn they have sufficient funding to cover their needs. The impact of finances might not be as large as many people think, however. A Health and Retirement Study by Boston College revealed that the effect of economic wellbeing on overall sense of wellbeing of retirees was relatively small.

The level of our health, on the other hand, has a major impact on our sense of well-being, and many retirees list this as key for a happy retirement. It is wise, therefore, to do what we can to maintain good health. Remaining physically active and eating right can help us stay healthy. Half an hour of walking per day, in some cases, has been shown to elevate our mood as much as taking antidepressants. Diets high in fruits and vegetables and low in saturated fats contribute to healthy bodies as well.

But diet and exercise are not a cure-all, and some health difficulties are beyond our control. Nevertheless, there are still ways of increasing happiness in retirement.

Study after study shows social contacts to be a major component of satisfaction in retirement. Retirees find that while they don't miss the stress of work, they do miss the society and support structure of their work colleagues. Some retirees maintain their contacts with their former colleagues. Some strengthen other existing relationships and create new ones. They find they have more time for children and grandchildren. But adjusting or creating social networks takes time. An extensive Harvard study revealed that the number one challenge for retirees was replacing the social connections that sustained them at work.

Having a purpose and making time for pleasure also contribute to happiness and wellbeing. Career coach Bill Ellermeyer says the happiest retirees he knows are engaged in meaningful activities. The overall purpose of these activities can vary widely and be big and overarching. Goals can be set to help achieve that purpose. Goals should be SMART: specific, measurable, achievable, relevant, and time-based. If we choose volunteering, it should be something that truly engages us, not something we do out of a grudging sense of duty. We can develop a routine that is related to our purpose and goals.

Time for pleasure can take many forms. We now have more time for the items on our bucket list. We can find or expand a hobby, eat out, pamper ourselves at a spa, spend time in a park or woods, travel, play brain games, take a course in a topic that interests us, or buy a pet. If we don't want the work of a pet, but would enjoy a furry friend, we can spend time with a therapy dog. There are 20,000 therapy dogs and handlers throughout the United States.

Taking time for pleasure is one way of nurturing a positive attitude. If we are people whose natural tendency is a negative attitude, it is possible over time to make an attitude adjustment. We can start by re-framing situations in a positive light—seeing the glass as half full, not half empty. Or we can make a daily list of blessings we are grateful for. That list can be just three items or ten items. The important thing is to do it daily. Practicing mindfulness can also brighten our world. For example, we can savor our food or notice the change in light throughout the day. We can close our eyes, breathe deeply, and focus just on our breathing for a couple of minutes. Or we can practice mindfulness by using apps such as *Calm* and *Headspace.*

The good news is that most retirees develop positive attitudes in retirement. In a recent poll, 82 percent of the responders said retirement gave them an opportunity to enjoy themselves, and 66 percent said they had a chance to have new experiences and to feel fulfilled.

Retirement is like a second adolescence. We can discover who we want to be as we grow older.

52 Commencement

Every new beginning comes from some other beginning's end. —Seneca

Like a school commencement, this chapter is both an ending and a beginning. Over a year ago, Editors Steve Woodhouse and Doug Calsbeek graciously said yes to my *Creative Aging* column in the *Marion County Express* and the *Sioux County Capital Democrat,* and a year of columns followed. I subsequently adapted those columns for this book.

The term "Creative Aging" doesn't appear in any of the chapters. But in 51 ways the chapters have covered the topic. Some were based on research and others rooted in my personal experience.

Perhaps you smiled at my resentment when I received my first issue of *AARP The Magazine.* Together we examined preparing for retirement and adjusting to it. We learned about ways to keep our brains sharp, and you may have smiled at the quip that a short pencil is better than a long memory. Together we explored the youth bias of our culture and age discrimination—in others and in ourselves. We learned about weathering loss, and chuckled about jokes such as "You know you're getting older when you're told to slow down by your doctor, instead of by the police."

We discovered that reminiscing can have a positive effect and a negative one. "Those were the glory days" can lead to dissatisfaction. "I conquered hardship; I can do it again" can inspire us to action. We learned about adjusting to retirement as a new stage of life, about the reasons time seems to go faster as the years go by, and about things that grow better with age.

We probably chuckled over outdated slang words from past decades. We lamented boondoggles with technology, and we rejoiced in small masteries of it.

I offered some tips on writing your memories and leaving a legacy for future generations.

You have seen me take a tumble, phone my junior high English teacher, play cards to win, and play crokinole for fun. You have witnessed my inability to nap, my difficulty parting with mementoes, and my brief burst of organized living. You have watched my husband and me nearly get taken in by a telephone scam.

During the year the column ran, column readers responded with emails, and I was grateful. Some of them told me they disagreed with my lack of interest in antiques. Others emailed me responses telling me of their own tumbles, and advised me how to avoid falling in the future. One of them emailed me memories of my mother as a rural schoolteacher before I was born. Some of them asked for the complete list of 50 ways to nourish their soul. One of them wrote about his volunteering, saying, "You will never find me on a front porch watching the world go by." They told me about sharing the columns with others, or others sharing the columns with them.

It was a rewarding year. But the *Creative Aging* well ran dry. And at the same time another well filled with water.

In April 2023, I heard Dr. Leonard Sweet speak at Pella's Vermeer Pavilion. He maintains that contemporary culture is a culture of story. He says that identity requires narrative form. His standard for items in his home: no item is allowed unless it has a story.

As I look around my home at the trinkets and knickknacks my husband and I have accumulated over the years, I realize that these items are not just stuff. They have stories. I also have stories not attached to things at all. I think the same is true for most readers who are part of my generation.

When the *Creative Aging* column ended, a new one began: *It Has a Story*.

Perhaps it, too, will become a book. Onward!

About the Author

In addition to her B.A. in English, Carol Van Klompenburg has an M.A. in theatre arts. She enjoys reading excerpts from her writing for groups. She has performed excerpts from *Creative Aging* and from two of her earlier books, *Child of the Plains: A Memoir* and *Tending Beauty: Forty Moments in My Gardens.* Carol lives in Pella, Iowa. Groups looking for entertainment are welcome to contact her at carolvk13@gmail.com.